A river
for all seasons

A river for all seasons

Tom Williams

Compiled by Fred Rashbrook

CASSELL
LONDON

CASSELL LTD.
35 Red Lion Square, London WC1R 4SG
and at Sydney, Auckland, Toronto, Johannesburg,
an affiliate of
Macmillan Publishing Co., Inc.,
New York.

First published 1980

ISBN 0 304 30555 3

Printed in Hong Kong

Contents

Acknowledgements

All the pieces in this book, ranging over a period of twelve years, originally appeared in *Angler's Mail* and *Angler's Mail Annual*, to whom the publishers would like to make grateful acknowledgement. The illustrations, specially commissioned for *A River For All Seasons*, are the work of Timothy Jaques.

Foreword

The Birth of a River-keeper

If you are an engine driver or a bus driver, doing the one thing in life you have wanted to do more than anything else, you probably owe the realization of that ambition to a spark put there by some person from the past. Perhaps it was a grimy fellow polishing a steam monster at Central Station or getting a faceful of fumes from a red double-decker.

The spark that led me to become a river-keeper was the late Ernie Leigh, a village bobby in the old sense of what a policeman in rural surroundings should be.

In a school life that was anything but happy I dawdled to school and ran the country lanes home to pond and lake, getting the bobby off his beat to supply hook and gut that enabled me to fish when all other recreation was controlled by the coal-mining children and village lads with no time for the game-keepering family. Who wanted to know the game-keeper's son when their father had been in court the week before for poaching a rabbit? Growing up in this sort of atmosphere you need a friend and I found him in the young village policeman.

Because of a little information on improving fishing that filtered through the *Game-keeper's Gazette*, I wheeled a barrow-load of lime into the artificial pond in the farmyard where I lived. The result was the death of all the big rudd that had been caught and caught and caught again until I knew each one individually. It was a juvenile attempt to alter the ph. in the water that went sadly awry.

Big Ernie, bicycle clips on handlebars and helmet on the grass when he was supposed to be on patrol, helped me restock. Small, undersized fish were gathered out of remote unfishable ponds until we had the basis of good fishing again. Then a 1 lb perch, carried on a bike through the newly opened Mersey tunnel in a half-full bucket of water (imagine trying to do that nowadays), was added to the other fish. That perch used to hover against the brick wall and if the sun got through the trees and lightened the shadows under the oak, you could surprise him and watch him fade into the depths. It was fishery management at its most elementary and enjoyable.

But I didn't always see eye to eye with the local Law. When caught with a pocketful of moorhen eggs I was made to walk back into the shallow lake margins along fallen trees and replace each egg more or less where I had found it. Then a few floats and lead shot found their way into my meagre tackle box as a sign that we were still friends.

Ernie had the idea that Halsnead Lake must hold some big eels. In an attempt to prove it dozens of night-lines were put out and baited with small rudd. Nuts and bolts served as weights. The line was laid in a circle at our feet, then, with a swing round the head, placed as near the middle of the lake as possible. It was my pre-school duty to pull each one in and re-bait, test the night's success, and, upon being released from school, to escort the bobby on a check that I had done my job.

I remember only two eels of fantastic size in several years of night-lining and that size has been exaggerated to something impossible by the passage of time.

When I grew older and had a bicycle of my own we would cycle out to those remote bits of water that dot the Lancashire watershed and catch fish—dusky tench and red-finned roach—where no one that we knew of had been before.

Idyllic days spent observing things that the townfolk's eyes would never see, taking in a wide-angled view that was centred on a float and being brought back to the angling of the moment by its movement.

All that time the comfortable fellow-fisherman was there with his unending supply of the odds and ends of tackle a young person needs—the first two-piece rod instead of a cane from the big house gardens, my first braided line (instead of thread from the work basket).

I also had the protection of the village policeman which, in those days, a game-keeper's son needed. Small wonder that when I game-keepered myself in later years I found the fishy side of estates a distraction from the feeding path that game-keepers walk.

As some sort of memorial to my old friend when he died, I approached the local school and talked the headmaster and some fifty pupils into forming an angling club, with a subscription of 50p to form a kitty, and then all the paraphernalia of much bigger associations—chairman, secretary and half a dozen honorary bailiffs—from monitors and prefects. A mile of carrier stream has been put on one side and a nominal rent of a couple of quid a year agreed on.

Because these youngsters' enthusiasms are new and have not yet had time to be one-tracked, they readily agreed that a different section of the school's activities should also have access to the water for boating and, if you like, just playing with water. If I can instil the sort of feeling that Ernie put into me into just one child per year I will regard this as a worth-while effort.

Part 1: Spring

The Obliging Pike

Now that spring seems to have arrived there is a gap between the end of coarse fishing and the start of the trout season that has left us with a sense of loss. It used to be filled by five beats of salmon anglers each with a guest, ten persons per day making an appearance and giving a feeling of companionship, a continuation of friends on the bank.

Now the salmon have ceased to venture so far upstream, those balmy early spring days have us looking for jobs instead of having the excuse of 'talking to anglers'.

Those anglers – sometimes I don't know just how to take them. Their priorities get so mixed up that I don't think they know their heads from their elbows.

Take one friend of mine who, in season or out, when he catches a trout, thumps it on the head and claims they taste just the same from the frying-pan whatever the time of year. Then the other day when we held an end-of-season pike match, he couldn't be persuaded that those pike taste just as well and should receive the same thump on the head.

Then there was this 28 lb pike and a conflict of ideas that went on for three or four days. It was caught and put back to live again. It was caught and went back for a second time, the weight varying a pound up and down on the two occasions.

Another angler saw it lying, with perhaps a touch of apathy, in the side of the river, a foot out from the bank, its aft-placed dorsal almost breaking the surface. A little agog at the width across the shoulder, the angler retreated, dropped the bait upstream, then dragged it slowly across the pike's vision.

Put yourself in that fish's position – it didn't really want to feed after the experience of the last week, so it must have been more or less a reflex action that caused it to open its mouth and, without moving the rest of its body, hesitatingly take in that herring and immediately spit it out again. But, alas, one hook of the treble caught.

It fought for its life for a third time. It was landed without the use of a gaff, put in a small empty trout-holding tank and there lived the life of an aquarium fish while its fate was discussed.

A fishing chef from Oxford did some calculations on the large number of French-type fish-cakes (*quenelles*), lobster-sauce

garnished, which it would produce. He sat on the rim of concrete for an hour with the offer of 30p per pound, which took the reward for a death sentence into reasonable figures.

We took it in a tank to The Bull at Downton, 200 gallons of water on the back of a lorry, and in the aftermath of a pike-fishing match, stood in circles with half-pints of lager and toasted the fish and draped it around with a dozen smaller pike caught during the day.

The young keepers and I, having had that pike in our possession for three or four days, began to feel a certain affection towards the stolid indifference that seemed to ooze from her. Admired the leap she gave, when, with a flash of the tail, she went three feet into the air, in an apparent grab at the throat of the angler who had caught her.

On the edge of the trout farm there is an old water-meadow set of hatches. Between them, lined with sandstone blocks and ancient brickwork, there is a pool much the size of a small town swimming-bath, though only carrying a couple of feet of water.

It has the usual residents of three chub, half a dozen roach and a few dace, plus one or two small pike lying towards the tail — minnow-gobblers, seekers after fry and never likely to grow much beyond their present weight.

Into this pool of clear water we put our big pike. Launched her as one would a ship, so that the momentum of the push gave her the drift that took her into the far wall. You could almost see the sense come back into her. The slow movement of tail and dorsal turned her slightly into the current, the head grey-coated from disturbed mud, the eyes peering upwards.

We left her alone for a couple of days and threw her a dead trout. She approached it like a retriever would a pheasant and with nose almost sitting on it seemed to change her mind and remember previous meals that had ended with so much fuss. She was in the same position, within a yard or so, the next morning. The dead trout was missing, as were several others that we had placed in her vicinity.

I saw her again this morning and she's gained a couple of small pike as escorts — pilot fish that lie on either side of her like the escorts of a battleship squadron, possible mates for some warm-water mating, maybe even a meal at the wedding feast.

We took an electric machine and ran it down an obscure carrier. Water shortage had narrowed the banks until the boat had difficulty pushing through islands of reeds.

We pulled out the chub from under the banks, plus 180 pike from 800 yards, most of them weighing around 20 lb to an ounce or so. There were also half-pounders by the dozen that must have been the food of the larger ones.

There seems to be a top-heavy over-balance of pike, for when fox eats fox there must surely be too many foxes. It would have seemed right to thump them on the head and adjust the balance.

Salmon Fever

I was here, there and everywhere, rushing around like a lunatic. A Wessex Authority man came to look at our water extraction plans, which to our mind were more circulation than extraction. Nevertheless everyone was willing to help, so down we went to the river in the car with my whereabouts left on the pad on my desk.

Salmon anglers of no experience were standing in the background waiting to get a word in edgeways amongst talk of pumps and millions of gallons per 24 hours and cubic metres of water, so that in the mind's eye you look at a hatch that falls to a lower level and in trying to square it into cube, see it in blocks like some crumbling edifice going through in granite lumps of solid water!

The fishermen waiting start to thread line through the reel, and I notice that it is not threaded through the spreader on the multiplier. I reach back and, taking possession of rod, line and reel, rethread it while still talking.

Two more anglers came up in the background, like a queue of people wanting to buy stamps in the Post Office while a personal conversation goes on behind the counter. At each lapse in the water flow and extraction talk, I was involved with a conversation over my shoulder with the demanding fishermen until I was given leave to attend them.

One of the sets of tackle being assembled belonged to the inexperienced one. The rod was six feet in length and as thin as a matchstick at the top end. Two silver-coated joints with a grip of barely 1½ inches, while at the line-winding end, a small hurdy-gurdy reel of child's dimensions loaded with 6 lb line.

He had read in some bygone book of 'thread-lining' for salmon, of a Mepps hurled into the distance, retrieved with the speed of a galloping horse and how if you set the clutch just right you could kill the largest fish.

The temptation was there to shoot him down as a leaver of baits in large Avon salmon, and then I remembered a long-gone friend of mine, Fisher-Crouch, and the pool below this cottage named after him.

I recalled his short pipe with a bowl no bigger than an acorn, sending out smoke like a destroyer belching to camouflage. Of his similar tackle to our friend's, of how at Avon Tyrell he killed a 36 lb May fish that for the first half-hour of a tug-of-war didn't even realize it was hooked.

'Twas only after being slowly pulled to the surface from the overhanging bank, and having to adjust its swim bladders to sink, that the salmon realized all was not right. It was landed and from that moment on, Fisher-Crouch wouldn't heed criticism of his tackle, and rightly so, for he used it with the expertise of graduation, starting with small fish and building up to that monster.

My own tackle: a one-ounce Wye lead mounted on the end of 20 lb braided nylon hanging from the end of a one-piece 9ft 6in salmon rod. Rubber button on the inside of the left elbow, thumb clamped on the reel, and so you instruct.

You demonstrate the half-turn of the body that uses the arm as an extension to the rod, the eye following the lead, rod tip lifted to swing a yellow Devon into the fast water under the bank, then the tip lowered to let a twisting bait hang for a moment under the nose of some imaginary salmon.

I did a short revision course for the four anglers, walked down the bank a pace or two and fished Barford stump, where the current whips off an old ash tree and pushes eddying water out into midstream. You can lift your thumb slightly and bump the lead along the bottom, knowing that the buoyant minnow is fishing a couple of feet below it.

Five of us fishing with one rod, downstream to the bend at Newcourt, a quarter-mile above Downton, where in the field behind us a landmine had blown a hole, now full of silt, which marks that particular salmon lie.

There was a sense of impatience among my companions, the sort of thing you see among children when one hogs the ball and the rest want to play. They should have known better than to let me have the rod, for there was a growing excitement as all my enthusiasms started to push to the surface.

The worries of water extraction and the gaining of the necessary licences, the gill troubles of several million fry, all this plus the fall of fish prices on the national markets – worries of everyday life were submerged in the knowledge that I was going to catch a salmon on the very next cast.

Down through the lie in slow one-foot strides, a cast each time I move my feet, each cast into midstream an exact length, covering the water with a searching Devon hovering the gravel bed. Down through the hole where I caught my largest fish ever, 31 lb of red April cock fish, and so relived for a moment that fight of some twelve years ago and the champagne lunch that followed (plus the whisky dinner of the same evening).

I fished on through the next quarter-mile. Through the Newcourt Willow, and Downton hatches, reliving a dozen fish caught and lost – acrobatic ten-pounders and dogged 20 lb-plus fish.

It was no surprise when I found I was on my own, that somewhere in the absorption of the past few hours I had lost my tail of impatient anglers who should have known better than to let me kick off and hope to stop me before noon!

Matrimonial Troubles

I don't think anglers realize the household repercussions that follow when they have dragged me out to The Bull for a drink. You know the sort of thing – there's a good cops-and-robbers programme on the telly, dinner is in the process of being digested, and there are soft lights and a happy feeling. But the angler in the pub, a long way from home, feels the need for company and calls me out. It's not that I need persuading, but oh dear, the matrimonial troubles that arise the following day.

But we are nothing like so argumentative as the rest of the

river valley travellers, and don't quite carry on to the extent the mink does. I was walking upstream from the Mill, a slow plod through the heavy mud left by the retreating water, when a black dog-mink struggled past in the opposite direction, his teeth firmly embedded in the neck of his mate and she making the sort of noise that is associated with things that go bump in the night.

Along the river margins they came, in and out of the water, ignoring the inquisitive nose of the Alsatian, and having a raging matrimonial row that awoke the surroundings to a feel of spring.

It couldn't have been all that bad for when he lost his grip she was after him in a flash and offered the nape of her neck for a fresh hold. Perhaps, like all females, the noise and struggle she made were all part of the game.

In similar vein, in the February moon, on a night so bright that shadows were solid in front as you walked, an otter crossed the weir whistling and moved upstream on to the shallows above Longford Castle, a bow-wave of speed that left dogs seeking the direction it had taken.

It whistled an invitation to its mate who answered from somewhere a mile upstream, a low hum of a whisper without strength, but penetrating in the result.

One shouted upstream, the other below, then a bow-wave along the left-hand bank rocked the edge, the hard arrow pushing downstream over the shallows. An eagerness to kiss and cuddle? Not a bit of it. They met in the middle of the shallows in nine inches of water like two packs of hounds dividing a single fox, and made more noise in the frost of a moonlit night than all the witches that sit in the local elms. To come so far, and let it be known that you are coming, there must have been an affectionate thought. This was only shown when two exhausted animals drifted down together beneath the Castle bridge and showed indifference to my presence.

In more sedate manner, ducks, or rather a duck, is nesting in the garden. She sits low in the flat, ivy-covered platform of an elm, ten feet from the ground and cocooned in feathers, sticks and the fresh growing ivy.

The drake mallard comes from nowhere in a low, flapping flight. He swims in slow circles, peering up to the unseen nest, and talks to her as ducks can in a wide variety of quacks – the soft cajoling 'Come down to feed', and the harsh, 'What the hell are you up to, it's time you left those eggs,' noise when his patience is exhausted.

A daily event, this, and I sit and watch in the happy glow of the ever-new occurrence.

Millions of Mouths to Feed

So many things happen in a year that when they come round again you have almost forgotten the problem. At present we are up to our necks in hatchery fry by the million.

Where the light catches the corner of the tanks there is a bloom of algae on the smooth blue fibreglass – algae that affect the water and put filaments on the gills of the fish.

So we dose with BKC, the same objectionable stuff that is used in swimming-pools to kill algae on the white tiles. Here the chemical is mixed with a detergent so that not only does it kill, it also washes and penetrates.

Young Andrew, with mathematical mind, is using a watering can, spreading the chemical mixture at two million to one. It slightly alters the specific gravity of the water making it easier to pick up rubbish from the surface.

With so many small mouths to feed there is a constant flow of trout fry food into the hatchery. Half a hundredweight divided by all those mouths with some sort of growth rate coming out at the other end.

In a morning preamble you try to assess how the fry are growing in this tank or that and try to sell them with a forecast of their weight a year hence. When Mr So-and-So phones and makes a guess of his needs in twelve months' time, your estimate of weight has to be reasonably accurate.

I manufactured a new system this year for my brownies. I persuaded Grice and Young of Christchurch to build a fibreglass tube, three feet wide and five feet tall, like a cannon from some previous war.

Into this we put windows of fine mesh copper with a water inlet at the base. Water turned on at a rate of 15 gallons per minute bubbles up through the centre, doubles back on itself and finally escapes through the perforated windows.

We introduced 40,000 brown trout of December hatch, January fed, and allowed them a moment to settle in and do their usual trick of congregating on the bottom, seeking the shade of each other to hide from imaginary predators that would have been more than real in the river.

The water was then turned on full; it blew them into a dispersed cloud and caused them to divide water-space between them. The advantage for the brownies is that it keeps them in the dark and stops the algae growing on the inside wall. At the same time it keeps any food introduced into the system in bubbling suspension, and pushes the lighter faeces out through the windows.

As fish-farming has progressed and the number of fry have to be divided among available spring water sources, we have sought new supplies by digging holes in water-meadows.

Behind the cottage, just across the field, I put a Hi-Mac in a pre-determined spot and dug down about twenty feet. I found a seam of gravel underpinning the silt of the meadow. That seam was so full of iron that the water precipitated out like cocoa after mixing with oxygen.

We put a diesel pump in and tried to clear it but at the end of hours of pulling water out it still came thicker each successive day.

It's always the place under your nose that has been before your eyes and in your mind possibly for years that comes up trumps in the end.

Adjacent to the fish-farm is a stone bridge with the date 1540 chipped into the stonework, a double-arched affair that apparently leads nowhere in the changing face of the countryside. Yet somewhere in the past, because of its robust construction, it must have carried traffic of importance.

Nearby was one of those beds of sedge that every farm grew, an acre of land that each year provided Norfolk reed that thatched the house of the Duncombe family.

Because it was low-lying and difficult to walk on, we thought that its water supply would be marshy and perhaps with a content of methane gas. We stuck the oxygen meter in it and saw it go off the dial in the reverse direction, registering almost nil per cent of saturation.

This raised such an interesting point that we sent a sample for analysis. Back came a high-level report of CO2. That raised an even more interesting point concerning the source of the water. CO2 does not stay long in water: it is the product of many things under the ground and goes along with a purity of source.

We dug a small hole five feet deep in a mixture of largish gravel and fine silt chalk and hit an underground stream of pressure that sent a million gallons per day sideways through the reed into the river.

Then we dug a channel to let it run more freely and watched the minnows enter the new stream, find the lack of oxygen, rapidly drift back and out again.

We put our diesel pump in and found so much clean water just beneath the surface that our eyes were like those of Klondike miners who had struck gold.

Now we are in a position to say what temperature the river must be; not the full flow of the river but say about five million gallons a day that could be fed to growing-on tanks.

We could mix cold water of January with warm spring water into a reasonable growing temperature. We could also balance the same two sources again in mid-June and July — cooling the high temperature of midsummer with this same constant temperature from the ground.

It brings a whole new phase into our river-keeping production line. We have dug out the channel by the old bridge and fashioned new tanks of concrete, laid a slab and bricked it off and dream of keeping temperatures in the healthy levels.

An interesting point about that old bridge: as we pumped the water out to concrete, so we revealed a wooden structure that had pegged the approaches to the bridge. Elm that was as solid as the day it was put in, but as it dried it became pulp and began to disintegrate, yet when we put the water back across it, it toughened into the hardness of new oak.

There were eels underneath and all those animals that had found the hollow woodwork a home out of the light. There was also an assortment of trinkets, clay pipes and old leatherwork.

The builders from all those years ago seemed so close, one wonders whether they were watching the newfangled equipment that was meddling with their ancient brick and woodwork.

The 'Mars Bar Kid'

We have a confectionery salesman who answers to the name of the 'Mars Bar Kid'.

Bob Windsor is one of those anglers who allows the sheer excitement of his hobby to overtake him. So Good Friday saw him lying full length on one of the caravan beds at the trout farm, suffering an alcoholic haze and murmuring, 'I caught a 23 lb salmon.' Repeating it over and over again till the lights were switched off in the early hours of the morning.

I remember the fuss a couple of years ago when at one of his first attempts at salmon fishing he landed a 12-pounder from above the Bailey Bridge at Charlton, a fish that was more photogenic than Elizabeth Taylor. It was held out at arm's length towards the camera lens, upside down, grasped by the tail, by the head, fingers in the gills, and with the angler standing nonchalantly with rod across his shoulders, or kneeling with the fish half submerged in the grass at his feet.

You can see that when Bob did this for a 12-pounder why the 23-pounder created this milestone.

Good Friday was a day of morning frost, when the early green of nettles on the riverbank was blackened by the morning cold. When the river temperature that had built back towards 50 °F took a severe knock during the day and went down as low as 45 °F. A chilly extra-pullover morning.

We fished until lunchtime – Ted Smith and I, and Bob Windsor, fishing the most unlikely water, trying, we suspect, to hook again the large rainbow he had landed out of season earlier in the year.

Ted landed four pike, two perch and an assortment of small trout that mistook the bright blue and yellow Devons for minnows migrating to spawn. I had a pull from a fish that brought itself to the surface and, wagging its head, tossed the Devon into the air, retiring to sulk in some inaccessible corner.

Ted, fishing in front at times and behind at others, kept up his pike-catching activities, fishing a little beyond the salmon lies into the stiller water of back eddies and increasing his catch with almost every other cast.

Ted had another beat to fish downstream on the Somerley Estate and there was some discussion during the lunchtime as to whether we should move down there and continue our pike-catching-cum-salmon-fishing exercise nearer the sea.

Bob joined us at The Bull and convinced me that the day wasn't worth it, that we would be better occupied having an extra pint and talking back into the memory of other days. Bob volunteered to fish instead of us and so, instructions were given to him to go to Ellingham Church above Ringwood, park by the bridge and fish beat three upstream.

Ted penned a little note to Colonel Crow and Wallace Tarry, so that these two stalwarts of Somerley would know the credentials of the fisherman.

Bob's tackle was not quite Somerley Estate. There was none of the professionalism that lower Avon anglers are equipped with. A lack of rod clips and multipliers, more an old carp rod and fixed spool reel, 12 lb monofilament line, a piece of wire instead of gut between lead and Devon.

And so Bob fished, and, as he had been doing in the morning, caught a pike and then several more before he snagged the river-bed, giving a sharp tug which broke the line where wire joined with lead.

Rebaiting with a Devon, he did an experimental cast upstream and on the downward swing through fast water hooked what he first thought was a smallish chub and then discovered he'd got a tiger by the tail.

No gaff, a rolled-up coarse-fishing landing net stuffed in the back of his jacket pocket, the handle fastened by two strings across the back, and down in the water, making attempts to bend his carp rod beyond its capabilities, was this silver salmon.

It was at this point, while Bob was struggling to unwrap the two disjointed rings of the net and wondering how the hell he was going to screw it into the shaft of the handle, that he spotted Wallace Tarry watching him in horror. You could see his mind working. Only four salmon caught on the Estate this year and the gods had been so destructive as to award a fish to this apparition.

If it had been me, I'd have put my hands over my ears, closed the eye that was pointed in that direction and walked away, trying to put the scene out of my mind for ever. Instead, Wallace unravelled the net, took off the restraining pieces of string and assembled it. Then with nerves at knife-edge, somehow got the tail of the fish into that small net and dragged it up the bank.

Bob Windsor's day was full. Wallace Tarry asked for the 'priest'. Bob, looking up at Ellingham Church, wondered what the local vicar had got to do with it, until it was explained with the help of a lump of fencing-post, the purpose of that instrument.

It is at this point that salmon anglers usually convey their appreciation to the keeper involved. A discreet rustling of a banknote as it is transferred from the wallet to the hand that is somehow handy for the act. Bob wasn't to know this, but he's a generous fellow and having had the fish carried to the car for him, offered Wallace the only thing that was available in this confectionery representative's car boot — a bag of Maltesers!

I've been given some strange things in my life — a two-bob tip from a well-known tackle firm director, a turkey and a set of wheels for my car, but never a bag of sweets. To Wallace's query of 'What shall I do with these?' Bob gave him a further duty: 'Distribute them among the local children.'

I would have loved to have heard Wallace's comments when he reported the fish to Colonel Crow later that day.

Nevertheless this Saturday sees the recumbent body of the 'Mars Bar Kid' slumbering the mid-morning away, the snores of his deep sleep blowing fumes that will need every window in the caravan opened. And repeated, like a record player stylus stuck in a groove — 'I caught a 23 lb salmon', going on and on.

As for me, I have a touch of the green-eyed monster. I've had salmon head and tail below me, then leap into the air at the sight of the Devon, do anything but take it in their mouths as a kindly act.

On the day that Bob hooked his fish I hooked a 12 lb pike in a deep run under the willows. The line went round a root and gave the impression of something much heavier fighting a dogged battle.

The disappointment was so great that I sent that fish when landed to Billingsgate and the money to the local Old Folk's Fund.

The Classless Sport

The river is still holding high but with a diminished amount of colour. It seems that at last all the accumulated silt from a low-water summer has been moved on and out of the way of the main flush of water.

Salmon fishing with a 9 ft 6 in rod pushed well out over the bank, you become aware that last year's low water allowed some of the riverside rushes to grow out and alter the shape of the river bank. Now it is established, this extra herbage will need several years of extra flow to push it back to its previous boundaries.

I fished the open Avon Tyrell water, with wind whistling downstream and ice forming in the rod rings. I fished a beat that so far this year has not produced a single salmon. Bigger, broader water than my own, it was totally unknown to me.

I had no idea of its spring holding lies, or the whereabouts of that dip in the bed that would encourage an early fish to lie, so I fished the unlikely and the likely with the same cold enthusiasm.

At the top of the beat was Tyrell's Ford where, legend has it, Sir Walter Tyrell fled across the river after slaying William the Second in the year 1100.

The ford, now superseded by bridges, is still crossed every few minutes by aircraft no more than a hundred feet up from the local airport.

When you think of the times we creep to avoid making a noise in case we frighten the fish or walk well back to stop our shadows crossing the water, then what fools the fish must be at Avon Tyrell, for they are caught despite large shadows crossing the water and in spite of the ear-splitting sound.

The day away from my own water stirred my bones to come home and attack again with renewed vigour my own lies and quiet corners, with negative result.

I got to thinking, as I sipped a morning cup of tea with one of my rods, what a great leveller of class and personality this sport of angling is.

This rod, a plasterer by trade, straight out of the London smoke, talked me through his last day's fishing, trot by trot, down a variety of swims, his eyes glowing with barely concealed excitement as he spoke of fish tearing line off the reel and the sudden lift of the rod tip as a good fish departs unseen to freedom.

I started the motor for him and watched the boat depart upstream to find a swim out of the wind.

The next angler into my fishing room is a famous author whose latest book, chosen by a Book Club as its reading for the month, is full of bits about rivers, flies and fishing. His heroes retreat to the country, as the author does, and fish as an escape from their supposed crimes in other places. Talking to him as we wander the bank I find myself trying to judge his mind and the value to him of this day on my water.

The next fisherman at my cottage walks in with tackle assembled, eager to be gone to some fancied back eddy under the willows. His pursuit, outside his hobby, is the delivery of bread around the supermarkets of a busy town. He carries with him into the country no less an active mind than the previous visitor. He organizes for me a visit to see the bread formed into rolls that stream unendingly through a continuous baking process.

An Admiral of the Fleet, slow and dignified in his step, greets me by name and with the same enthusiasm of any other of my fishermen. We fish the morning through to the lunchtime break. I am invited down to see the Fleet, to attend the dockyard gate at a given hour and be the Admiral's guest.

I accept and am the guest of the Royal Navy for the day. I am escorted through the bowels of an aircraft carrier, then shipped out across the bay to wander the depths of the Navy's largest battle-wagon.

The only connection between me, who during my war service never rose above the ranks, and my illustrious host, is the river bank. There is no master – servant relationship between those who walk the river within the common bounds of angling. Bread-roundsman, plasterer, even an ambassador to a foreign court, are all equal within a common interest.

Time for Contemplation

When the coarse fishing season ends, the salmon angling programme plods on alone for a while then, come April, the trout fly season joins in and the two types of angling march on together. To a person like me, who is an habitual gate-leaner, it's perhaps the most wonderful time of the year.

A hatch of fly moves downstream following the surface currents, turning round in the eddies and then going on again, catching a gust of wind so that their sails touch the surface and, like a yacht, become waterlogged, fluttering until the great neb of a big trout pokes out of the water and, despite its size, takes without the hint of a splash.

Dark olives, joined by the occasional mayfly, patches of grannum sprinkling the water like nutmeg on a custard then, as the light fades, the evening hatch of blue-winged olives. A time to gate-lean and water-watch.

I like to sit behind one fish and renew a yearly acquaintance. To hook him and put him back and go there again and, because his education is taken a step further, try and overcome his shyness by pulling him into the net once more.

I never upset their dignity by handling or by spreading them out on the grass by the side of the reel and photographing them. The hook is levered free and their return to the water is a matter of a gentle push out towards midstream.

The posh sort of fishing of the Test and Itchen is all very well. You dress in the demanded uniform and wave the prescribed rod made by the right people, but it is too artificial to help a mind that requires relaxing, unless that is, you are still caught up in the thought that this is in fact the thing to do. Fish 'drey fley' as Harry the Boat would say.

I saw him a couple of days ago worming the weir. He landed a good trout, so he paused and, knowing he must return it, completed a full circle by slowly turning on his heel, peering over the top of his glasses looking for me. Not seeing the shadow in the wood, he thumped that trout on the head and put it into his tackle-box, faster than I had ever seen him move before.

But I get off what I was saying. If you follow the gang and do the accepted stretches on your lawn-like river bank, half the fun of the thing is lost. Far better to take a light, 8 ft rod, a child's fixed spool reel loaded with 4 lb line tied direct to a Stewart tackle and the only other equipment — a couple of score of worms off the lawn.

I know a dozen streams no wider than a yard that are ignored even by the children, yet if you drop a worm into the head of each tiny pool, there are ½ lb trout waiting under the bank for just such a thing.

These tiny brooks are everywhere. They are overgrown with the remnants of the last three years' docks and nettles, yet in places they have water three feet deep and you couldn't drown a mouse in their shallows.

Where the trout population comes from is a mystery. Perhaps it is the progeny of a sea trout run that got into these brooks on a spate and found a home to their liking, or even the native browns living there unsuspected for hundreds of years.

I once fished such a stream, working my way up, letting the bait run beneath bushes so that I was fishing out of sight in a tunnel of brambles. I had a farm labourer laughing at the apparent silly season for anglers, yet wiped the grin off his face with a half-dozen fish that wouldn't have disgraced Mick Lunn on the Houghton water.

Then, of course, there is always the surprise when you find a hole inhabited by a 'grandfather' that tears round in his restricted beat and busts you from the sheer unexpectedness and violence of his movements.

Such a fish will be there at the end of the year and there again the season after, something to look forward to, a renewing of a personal battle of wits that is the same thing as my old favourite brownies here on the main river.

I have the feeling that you shouldn't take without putting back, so it is a simple thing to take twenty or thirty brown trout fry and drop them in so that perhaps you may not have a bad day at some future time.

Brown trout fry are easy to come by — you can get a thousand for £5 and a couple of pounds'-worth will fill your sink with a black moving shoal.

The other day one of my fishermen tried a slow bend that isn't usually attractive to salmon anglers. He bumped his lead round in a wide semi-circle, feeling the river-bed, bumping so that his wooden minnow floated attractively a yard behind and six inches up. This in a stretch of river that no salmon had been known to pause in.

Suddenly his lead failed to find the bed and the angle of the line entering the water steepened. A fish took, fought well and a clean 17 lb springer was grassed.

We all like to find new lies — that is, spots on the river-bed where, as the salmon come upstream, they pause, then turn and try the currents for size and see if this is the spot that reminds

them of their youth in the river.

A 17-pounder was followed the next day by a 14-pounder and then an 18-pounder, confirming that this tiny bathtub of a hole was just what the doctor ordered as a salmon-holding place.

We have marked it on the map and each day the angler on that beat sizes up his cast and swings a bait through the lie. Now a name is needed so we all sit round a pint and argue.

Basically it is featureless – two river banks and a flat surface of water. There's a willow tree two hundred yards away but we already call another pool by that. Then somebody remembered the local village's bomb damage and at that spot a wartime crater.

We all have ambitions to have a pool named after us, especially if we found it and the first fish was a good 'un, but I don't think we will ever beat the 'Bomb' as a name for this one.

'Nog' Declares War

When I was a game-keeper I used to dream of seeing the last carrion crow and rat pass in front of me while I blasted them into oblivion with both barrels of the twelve-bore. Then I would think of the ease of rearing my pheasants. Woods full of happy guns blazing away to their hearts' content.

I never thought that I would get a similar fixation about looking after fish, for after all, don't they hide under the water and isn't the depredation from pike a reasonably easy thing to contend with? Hasn't that pike got a dislike for fast, streamy water and the well aerated shallows of the chalk stream?

I forgot the heron, 'Nog'. No one would suspect that the one lonely sentinel, the grey-hooded Nog, would become gregarious and gather himself into gangs with more malice in their minds than the city yobbos. Through the autumn and winter months there was a breaking-up of those feathery gangs so that we viewed the one or two intruders at the trout farm with tolerance, and the promise that we would look to him should he come too often.

We felt sorry for him during the winter when the lakes froze and the minnow shoals retreated into the mud. Whatever weight he carried on his angular frame, we didn't mind the occasional trout that fuelled the warmth in his bones.

At Salisbury there is a heronry of about seventy nests, two birds to a nest, three eggs brooded, a possible total this coming July of more than three hundred birds — and that's just one heronry of more than a dozen within a twenty-mile radius.

A plentiful supply of fish kept the heron stock high, and so in the spring they collected and laid their eggs, and the cock heron joined with other mates and descended on the fish farm in one grey blanket — a hundred birds with a mass intelligence system.

One hops forward a hundred yards, there is a slight, almost imperceptible nod and another heron flies on the next hundred yards, while the pack waits in the background. The leading bird settling near a trout stew resists the temptation to feed until he gives the all clear, then in comes the gang.

If you try to hide from a heron by sitting still, forget it. Build a hide with a pillar-box slit across the middle and they take a week to accept it as part of the landscape. Poke the barrel of a twelve-bore through the slit and this unnatural movement is enough to have them scurrying in all directions.

And so the fight goes on. Late night and early morning, through the dark hours into morning mist, until such time as there are people about. All this while the hen bird sits inviolate on her eggs, awaiting the cock bird's return with food for the broody Mum. When the eggs hatch, the hen joins in the general fish-farm attack.

We are in no way winning. Numbers are added to each day and trees are occupied in a wide circle, watching for defences to drop and the weary eyes of young keepers to slacken through a lunch-time cup of cocoa. It is common to count sixty birds in the air at once and do a sum quickly in the mind of £1 per visit and several hundred quid a week lost.

I read somewhere that there's a gentlemen taking heron eggs and rearing the results as one would a dozen chickens, stocking parts of the country where there's a lack of grey fishers. Would that he would come and take his eggs from our heronry!

The Close Season Controversy

I have been reading some bits and pieces about whether we need a coarse fishing close season or not. Some of the argument is sound but an awful lot of it is written by people who should know better.

Those who advocate fishing for one species through the complete year cannot know the change in physical make-up and habit that takes place in the majority of fish when they spawn. I know that the present close season does not cover the complete spawning period, but to the species it does not cover it gives a chance to recuperate in peace or prepare for the act without having to fight to the point of exhaustion.

Two of my anglers fished on the last day of the season among a shoal of roach. Not understanding the strange lumps and bumps on the snouts and sides of the fish, they knocked them on the head and buried them.

Both these gentlemen were anglers of many years' experience, yet they had never seen a roach in spawning garb before. They agree that it would be wrong to handle fish at this time.

Of course there must be a close season. Think how vulnerable roach are when they gather in those vast shoals to clean themselves after spawning. I know that the fast water below our main hatches is full of these hungry fish at the end of April and the beginning of May. They must be allowed some time to disperse back to their own holes and corners.

Two hundred chub with their backs out of the water is a common sight on the fast shallows at the end of May. It seems necessary to them at this time to recover like that. Were they to be disturbed, something would be upset in their life-cycle and within a year or so we would begin to wonder what had happened to them.

March 15 does not come too soon for the perch. If the season were to go on for another week you could sit over any deep hole on this river and pull perch dripping with spawn on to the bank all day.

For those who want heavy keepnets, no matter what the cost, or the income from a fishing let with no thought of the future, that's fine. But the majority of us who would conserve to enjoy later, should speak against this talk of doing away with the close season.

I have all sorts of anglers — good ones, bad ones, untidy ones, good-natured ones, and Harvey.

Harvey comes to the house and says, 'I'll take a boat.' My heart sinks, so sometimes does that boat. It will take a month to recover from his visit. He coats each oar handle with half an inch of thick groundbait, stuck so as to be uniform all round. Harvey's mixture, from a secret formula, sets like concrete, moulding the form of his fingers as it does so. We clean it off knowing that on his next visit he will replace it.

He puts a tin of maggots in the warmth of the fishing room and leaves my wife to find a rope of wriggling creatures circling round the skirting-board, under the door and into the sitting-room. When his attention is drawn to the upside-down tin with its perforated lid, he gives a little grin that charms the Missus and is allowed to bob his way down the garden without a word of reprimand.

When warm summer months come, there is a permanent big blue fly buzzing in the fishing-room window. When the window is opened and the blue fellow pushed out to feed the hawking chaffinches, two more flush from the reservoir that Harvey has carefully nursed through the winter months.

The mystery of this constant supply was solved when Harvey's fishing jacket, left at my home for his convenience, was found with its pockets full of chrysalises, all either hatching or about to.

When one of my boat anchors was missing, it was Harvey who had failed to tie it on before he threw it overboard. When his attention was drawn to his misdemeanour, he grinned, stripped the clothes off his seventy-year-old frame and spent an hour or so rooting round the bed of the stream. He recovered the anchor and in the process shocked the village ladies for, of course, Harvey did not bother with swimming trunks.

His biggest crime is that he is a con-man of the first order. Attention is what he wants, someone to hold his hand while he fishes. Over the years, anglers of all sorts have shown him the finer points of the game and have then found themselves fishing for him while he leans back with half-closed eyes, apparently giving his closest attention. In truth, he is fishing without the effort of holding the rod.

An indignity that I suffer is that sometimes I am asked: 'Why don't you give that poor old man some help?'

Yet because he has fished and had his fun for seventy years or so, because he would be the first to help a novice with sound advice, even the loan of his last piece of tackle, 'he' is my friend.

The river would not be so alive without Harvey.

The Salmon Enigma

Oh, to be a river-keeper now that May is here. All thoughts of cold winds are swept aside with the river and the surrounding countryside bursting with life.

Ugly crawling nymphs and caddis swim drunkenly to the surface, burst out into the air with wings of gossamer and bright glossy colours down their length. Dace fry fill the eddies, rippling the surface like hidden showers of rain, while on the bank yellow patches of kingcup and newly emerging water iris splash the water meadows with the brightest colours that Nature can paint.

We have a colony of yellow wagtails as bright as any canary, and far more lively than their grey-backed cousins. There are redshanks nesting, and a lone greenshank, with its different, high-pitched call, passed through last week. Each successive warmer day moves salmon higher up-river with far more impetus than a sudden spate.

There is a smattering of mayfly and a start to the evening rise. All this is missed by the grayling, for he alone is digging up the shallows and burying eggs that should have been disposed of a week or two ago. But it would be a strange year if something or other didn't quite follow the pattern of May.

I have often wondered how, or why, salmon vary so much in the things they do. I was lucky enough the other evening to latch into a clean 23-pounder that disappointed in the fight she put up. She took with a bit of a bang, having followed a yellow Devon across the river, taking it deep under my own bank. She bent the rod and paravaned out into midstream. After a few moments of both of us pulling in opposite directions she came in like a lamb, was gaffed and dispatched all within a matter of ninety seconds. Perhaps a clue to her inability to make an effort to escape lay in the fingernail-sized sea-lice that spotted her flanks.

Experienced gillies from lower downstream would say that

these miniature creatures, with their long ray-like tails, lose that tail thirty-six hours after leaving the salt, and that the rest of the sea louse falls off after another twenty-four hours. So perhaps there would be an excuse for this fish being tired if it had travelled the twenty-nine miles from the sea to my beat, at the same time having navigated eight separate sets of hatches – none of them a straight jump and swim affair – and then having to fight for its life, all within a matter of little more than forty-eight hours.

Early on in the week I caught a 12-pounder that went berserk the moment it felt the hook. It cartwheeled in several directions at once, its runs were twenty or thirty yards long, first across the river then backwards and forwards down and against the current. Never have I been so glad to pull a fish on to the grass as that one. It had the slightly stale look of a fish that had been in the river a matter of weeks – red blobs on the gill covers and tinge of red about its general appearance. This fish must have made a comfortable journey and conserved its strength, though in the end it didn't survive any better than the 23-pounder.

I had a short sharp hard fight with another salmon that took up a traditional site under our Castle Bridge. From the upstream side of the bridge I lowered a Devon, dead in line with where the fish lay, lowering it inch by inch at the commands of one of my watching fishermen, until the spinning bait was a foot in front of the fish's nose.

It edged forward, opened its mouth and apparently took the Devon in. My friend shouted, 'He's on,' but from the upstream end of the fishing-rod there was no response at all.

I tried gently tightening, but all I got back was my bait. This happened many times until we hit upon the ploy of giving the fish slack line as soon as it had the bait in its mouth. This did the trick, for the fish backed away, tightening into the hooks.

That fish did a couple of dives in different directions and the hooks lost their hold. Now, what worries me is, how many times, when we are out salmon fishing, do fish mouth the Devon without our ever knowing?

Old Friends

Five children and a fibre-glass boat, a six-foot floating platform for their enjoyment – as I write they play, paddling beneath branches overhanging the water, almost on nodding terms with a friend of mine, a carp who allows me to walk past him without sinking into the shadow of the trees.

If I pause and consider him, I realize that he has a slow process of thought that is as predictable as a timetable. A slow sculling of fins, then a drift into deep water, even a disturbance of mud if I bend in his direction. A fish that understands folk, knows what we are about. A fish that can tell a baited hook from a free-floating piece of bread a mile off. An intelligence to match that of the angler.

On the river, I know of half a dozen fish that I can say are on nodding acquaintance, fish that I look for when I pass that way. Large brown trout that have grown in the river, perhaps hatched from parents that have belonged to the valley for more years than old-established families. Certainly grown in size in the water, not put there with stew-bred habits.

In this fishing for stew-bred trout let no one compare large rainbow with the large wild brownie. Such a fish of unknown size has lived off the corner of my garden for several years. He paid attention to no one, didn't change his habits when large pike sat in the deeper water below him, and when the river turned brown – as it used to do from high rainfalls – he moved into one of those water-meadow drawings and didn't change habits one iota.

I used him as a whipping-boy. I would point him out to some would-be fly fisherman and leave him casting to the impossible for hours on end. The trout, joining in the game, would dimple to some invisible insect just when enthusiasm began to die.

Fishermen can be classed into as many different categories as you like to divide them, with the 'over-expert' expert placed closer to the duffer than some of those in between. Then there's the man apart who is none of these things, who if put on some well-fished North Country canal would scratch his head and doze through the day. Yet give him a single fish to stalk and he will spend the year weighing up the angle of angling, only casting his bait when circumstances allow for success.

Ted Smith and I walked past the bottom-of-the-garden brownie and, as is our habit, stepped aside and passed the time of day with him. We watched him cope with one of the largest hatches of grannum I have ever seen, a million small sedges coming off the water in brown clouds and crawling up the cuffs of our jackets and roaming down socks and shoes.

The trout, higher in the water than normal, was opening its mouth and taking those hatching nymphs that came down in line, not moving sideways half an inch to take the small mouthful. In the past we had seen the wave of his feeding run shift minnow shoals through the surface, push dace before him like a sheepdog. This was the first time we had seen him take a nymph.

It was one of those sunny days that seemed to go on, unending, windless, warm beyond the time of year, when the watching of fish is a drugging pastime that bends the mind into reasonable paths of sane and tranquil thought. Shall we try him with a fly, a fine cast with a green tipped March Brown to try and deceive? It was but a matter of minutes to put up a rod and strip off a length of light nylon, to wave the line to the given length and to drop a leaded nymph eight inches in front of his nose.

We watched it sink and saw the mouth open and all in that moment things happened. A cartwheeling rush across the surface, all tail and fins, the screech of a reel that was never meant to run so hard against the ratchet. Then, with all the shock and surprise ended, the dour wandering of a fish that seeks some sort of refuge.

Was it an hour or just a minute. Perhaps only a moment between the net and the hooking, a gap of time that seemed to be all excitement and guessing at weights. We thought of him as 6 lb or thereabouts, maybe seven at a push, but when I tried to get him head first into a small trout landing net, the centre of balance was on the outside and it was with some difficulty that he was landed.

'Put him back,' said Ted.

'Knock him on the head,' was my verdict. For this cock fish turned the spring balance a little below 10 lb and there was that ragged look about him that said he was on the downward slide in life. Left in the river to recover from this hard fight might have meant a slow death from some accidental disability. The grasping fingers that went in his gills when the net failed to hold him had sent a mist of blood into the water and so he was despatched, taken to The Bull and admired.

I walked towards the same stretch of river this morning and

felt the loss of a friend. I walked down to the hatches at Stanlynch and kicked the pipe that drains the stockfish pond. I watched a couple of trout drift backwards into the main river and, in the light of a new-found guessing at weights, lifted their apparent size by three or four pounds and set to planning a day.

On the way home, on the corner at the bottom of the garden, another trout has taken up station, a smallish fish of perhaps three or four pounds, one that must have lived in the shadow of its elder and had now come out into the sun.

Anything Can Happen

That Monday morning feeling is usually unknown to river-keepers, but I had more than a touch of it when a ten o'clock-starting angler came back to my door at ten-thirty complaining that he was unable to fish his beat because there was a dead cow in the middle of the shallows.

Couldn't he fish round it, I asked? But it wasn't so much that the cow was dead as the length of time it had been dead. In fact it had obviously been in that condition for a long time. With the use of a long rope and a tractor driver reinforced with Scotch, we got the current behind it and sent it on its way.

When you start a Saturday in that fashion and have the rest of the weekend still before you then anything can happen.

I suppose the trouble with dry-fly men is that they require a lot of water-room. A passing swallow can put a fish down so anything larger is looked on as an intrusion into the holy of holies, unless that intruder can talk trout and is dressed in the uniform of the day.

Would I move on a picnic party? They were on the best piece of water and children were paddling, bless 'em. I can be nice to family groups when the need arises, as it did on this occasion. Two Amazon ladies, five young Tarzans and a pathetic man.

None of the children was over eight and in a passport description of British male/female child blue would have fitted the lot. May water temperatures were still in the low fifties.

They didn't lift their heads as I approached; even the dogs didn't get their usual good-doggie pat and at my 'You are not allowed here,' opening speech, the children took to the water like a brood of ducks chased by a stoat.

The angler whose beat it was winced and in a look conveyed to me that wasn't it just where the water came out of the deep on to the shallows that good trout always took up station? It was plain that the blame for this interference had been shifted to me.

Maiden aunt out with Mum and Dad as children's help, mouth full of buttered roll, wanted to know who I was, hand lifted to silence about-to-speak pathetic male. I told her. 'Who employs you?' I told her and where he lived. She promised to report my threatening behaviour. The children left the water and were issued with a roll apiece as they came up the bank. They gathered round as an Old Bailey jury, mouths working, eyes squinting up at me.

They wouldn't move and the beat owner couldn't or wouldn't fish. If only the dogs would growl just a little. With no help from that quarter I went down to The Bull and had a pint. After all, that angler still had most of his beat devoid of picnickers and arguing with maiden aunts is not altogether in my line.

In the afternoon I went out with an angler who fished like a lunatic yet still hooked two salmon. It's true he lost them both, but that was probably because I was hanging round his neck trying to get him to do the right thing. Left to his own devices he could well have landed both, but probably wouldn't have hooked them in the first place had I not been there. At least that is what I told myself as I got to thinking what time the bar opened again in the evening.

Sunday wasn't a lot better, if at all; more anglers turned up than usual, earlier than usual. Jobs that should have been done weren't completed. Some of the fish didn't get their early meal. I had a mental picture of 10,000 pairs of eyes gazing up through the surface looking for that friend who, come rain, hail or frost, brings their breakfast.

Doubling up on some beats meant that rods who wouldn't normally speak to each other had to fish together, so instead of the usual 'Thank you for the beat,' I got dull, mumbled, half-buried threats as they retreated.

An old lady whose house overlooks my fry stews collared me when I did arrive to feed. 'One of those beautiful big grey birds has been flying between your pond and the middle of that field.'

On the stew about fifty four-inch trout lay dead, some in the water, others inert on the bed, while in the middle of the field some three hundred small bodies were piled up waiting to be collected as feed for young herons in nests a mile away – the overload on a flight path from pond to high timber.

At lunch, fishermen complain of half the canoes in the country boating through their beats, of lorry-loads of cut weed making life unbearable.

The canoeist was the vicar's son doing a 'Steptoe' for tackle caught on trees, and the weed no more than that broken off by swans feeding on the shallows. Feeling out of tune with everybody I cried, 'Enough,' packed a pair of socks, press-ganged my two sons on leave from the Navy to take over, then bolted for the back-end of Dorset.

A Job With Potential

Of all the ambitious anglers who write to me saying they would like to do similar work on the river, none mentions wanting to be the driver of a fish delivery lorry, yet this is obviously the finest fishery position in our industry. You visit streams, lakes, rivers and ponds, and are allowed an insight into the stocking and culling policies of each fishery, plus an invitation to a couple of days on the very best of the water, at your convenience. Now who among you ambitious anglers has ever thought of the vast fishy potential of such a job?

I delivered a load of fish to one of those tiny chalk streams that criss-cross the chalk countryside, backed the lorry up to the water's edge and sprinkled the fish into tiny clear pools. Standing in the background were half a dozen anglers false casting in anticipation. They could hardly wait for the vehicle to leave the waterside. I hung around and watched them flog a frustrated couple of hours without a rise. It would seem that newly released fish need a little time to get back into the stew habit of grabbing anything that moves in case another gets there first.

On a beat of a well-known chalk river with a 150 million gallons a day flow, we had the laborious job of carrying fish in dustbins about half a mile before the owner was happy with the release spot. As the dustbin was lowered into the river and the water gradually infiltrated the fish, there was a tremendous splashing swirl as pike took the first trout that headed for liberty.

A pike of about 15 lb drifted backwards in the clear water with a 2 lb trout held crosswise in its jaw, while another pike of almost equal dimensions edged forward to take the next of the unwary fish.

The fish that hadn't been released were hurriedly lifted from the water and an almost demented fishery owner rushed back to his lodge in search of a suitable pike remover. A couple more 'drops' on that beat both had pike waiting for their meal. No wonder there was the need for stocking.

I took another load to one of those new lake complexes, watched the fish swim away into their new home, then, in a patch of summer-like warmth, sat and watched the fish rising way out in the middle of the new water. When these lakes are planned, the planners can pick the type of countryside they are sited in. In this case it was rolling Dorset Hills.

There was a litter of fox cubs playing alongside the hedge above the water and fallow deer drinking at the new water-hole. There were badger marks in the new mud and an air of a piece of real country. Anglers in such surroundings are fortunate beings, despite the 'tame' fish.

There is a grey wagtail's nest in the long grass on the edge of the fry pond and it has amused us to watch one of the parent birds collecting insects off the water surface in an attempt to feed its young. Amused us until we found a dozen inch-and-a-half fry round the margins of the nest. Watching it hover over the water, it was soon apparent that this miniature hawk was taking fish as they lingered near the surface. Further nesting sites are being discouraged in that area!

It's amazing the number of creatures that become predators when small trout are available. We had a water-shrew that lived in the corner of the hatchery shed and stored enough tiny bodies to last him a year before the smell led to his discovery.

Then there are the wren and the robin. Both of these, when conditions are right, are not above helping themselves to our so-called 'well-guarded' fish. Still I suppose it's fair enough – they don't understand in their little feathered heads the economics of the situation.

Mayfly Memories

There are peaks of excitement in any sport. Maybe it's a Wembley Cup Final if you are a football enthusiast. To me, it's mayfly time on the Itchen.

'Twas said twenty years ago, and many times before, that the hatching insect has a certain smell, and that if you listen closely enough, their million sweeping wings have a sound in still air that people have tried to write about and lost themselves in the description.

'Come and have a day,' is so often said when there is little time to go, but nevertheless it means a day on the Itchen, back among wild brownies and the occasional mayfly-taking salmon. A choice of two beats, one down near Eastleigh with more salmon, the other up in the unstocked stretches where the River Arl meets the brook water.

The lower water was a disappointment. Local poachers had to be driven protesting from the water and even then, with a 10 a.m. start, they claimed the bank rights from daybreak, perhaps even before that, for all we know.

On the upper Itchen where four-to five-pound brownies would take up residence in a small eddy under the bank, a place where hatching mayfly circled twice before catching the main current, a moving collection of scum and other rubbish shared the same water and in the middle of it, the smallest possible dimple of a rise. A breaking of surface tension plus the sort of noise Kojak would make with his lolly.

Alas, that was yesterday. It was how I remembered it when the water was shared with the social few, when Air Marshals vied with Judge-on-Circuit in the lateness of their start. When it wasn't a case of looking for a taking trout, but which one and how many. When flies were tied with upright wings and resembled a fly instead of a stickleback pulled backwards by the tail.

Must we talk of disappointment or pretend that our exclusive right to fish could not compete on a competitive fishery?

First there was a lack of mayfly and just a trace of detergent scum from the upstream fall. There was a hatch of Iron Blues, that morsel of fly life that, if you taste it accidentally in a downstream wind, puts a strain on the back of your throat in your haste to get rid of it. But to a trout it must be something extraordinarily good, for he deserts all other fly, even the mayfly, when the Iron Blue hatches.

The Iron Blue is a strange insect in that it will hatch when there is a ripple on the water. It has the strength, or streamlining, to resist the wind and hang in mating clusters in any shelter. At hatching time you can see a fish chase it out of the water, while in its spent condition at dusk it more than competes with the B.W.O. as the meal of the day.

On this day of days, and disappointments, I fished on into the dark, watched the few mayfly left to the river hatch and lose themselves in riverside bushes. Insufficient of them for the trout to realize they were food.

I caught several three-quarter-pound fish and a stocked rainbow from a previous year that in the water looked all of 6 lb, but could have been tied in a knot as a result of its wasted slimness. A cock fish with milt still issuing from the vent, unfulfilled in this brownies' 'Paradise Lost'.

Back home it has been a week of weed. Somewhere upstream they have been skating across the gravel with a keen knife, trimming out all the river-weed in an over-abundance of enthusiasm for the job. Clogging every hatchway and weed-rack and causing thirty miles of salmon anglers to stand and watch. It has been coming through in the night and early morning and rises to a river-covering raft just after lunchtime.

Nobody seems to go home for dinner or even sleep and the telephone lines have been hot with complaints to the Water Resources Board Fishery Officer in an avalanche of misery.

It was inevitable that as the trout stretches upstream of Salisbury died and coarse fishing rights became more available, they should rake the weed out to provide a swim and clean up the water before the mid-June start.

Ten million minnows migrating. A band of life in spawning garb as round, black and thick as a ten-inch plastic pipe, half a mile long. All moving in concerted effort upstream, breaking in panic at each drive of a trout, flashing across the surface at any passing shadow. They go into the trout farm and through the screens among the captive trout. They, recognizing fish fingers 'on the hoof', waste their energies chasing this elusive morsel.

I watched them for ten minutes or so and every now and again one would lose its sense of life, wriggle like a spun minnow and be gone. These minnows feeding on the remnants of the trout food take droppings and fish-feed dust as part of their diet, growing in size and passing on that food-gathering ability in a single tasty mouthful. We killed a 4 lb trout and his bulging tummy wriggled with still live minnows. It made one wonder why he should even consider the small inert nymph that he took.

In the dark, when fear of deeper water hits these tiny migrating fish, they crowd into the shallows and run the overflows to the upper levels, jumping one-foot falls like miniature salmon and miraculously finding a way through fast water. There must be something special about the minnow for so many survive and so many die.

A Wonderful Day

I recently had the privilege of acting as the 'eyes' of a man who had lost his sight as a result of enemy action during the London blitz.

I had been told, before he arrived, that this old gentleman had been an angler of great promise and that this occasion was going to be his first day's angling for many years.

He turned up at my house with his driver very early in the morning; in fact, so great was his enthusiasm that he and his driver had had to park down the road to wait for daybreak.

His tackle was old. A Nottingham reel with linen line that had long since gone past its useful life. His spinners and Devons were eroded and rusted, their hooks barbless and crumbling. He dug into a huge box of assorted baits and emerged triumphant with what looked like a lump of old wellington boot: a piece of rubber tied round with wire. He felt for my hand and said, 'We'll start the day with this.'

This hookless lure had obviously died in the depths of that long neglected tackle box, but from the way it was handled, it evoked all sorts of memories in my friend's mind. A new start obviously had to be made, so a braided Terylene line was taken from my cupboard and whipped to his reel. Rotted, faded gut casts I carefully packed back into a very dry damping tin. All this time his rod was held firm, pointing towards the river and waiting to be off. What was the river like? Was there plenty of water?

Were the trees out in leaf and was there a haze of fly dancing in the shadow?

All those things that we take for granted he wanted to know.

Equipped now for the job at hand, we moved to the river. Never have I fished with anybody with such enthusiasm. His timing could not have been better.

We worked our way downstream. I had to describe each foot of the way, each sound had to be named, every bird described. A fish, disturbed by the passing line, heaved itself out of the water, splashing down on its side with a tremendous thump. Poised like a spaniel and shivering with excitement, my companion got to within a pound or so of my estimate of its weight.

A woodpecker rattled away in the woods across the river, and at each burst of noise all fishing stopped so that it could be enjoyed. I never realized before how a cock pheasant crowing is so perfectly in tune with a woodpecker.

The early spring sunshine seemed to provoke every river valley sound, bringing to life the water meadows as I have rarely known them. In my own world of the riverside I was led to and taught a better appreciation of my surroundings.

A couple of hours of this and I was seeking a better way for my companion to fish, so I loaded him into a fishing punt and poled away downstream. This was easier. The toe of his boot in the front of the boat gave him a direction in which to cast, while at the stern I dragged the weight behind, holding back over all the likely spots.

We hooked the bank a few times and one or two trees had baits left on them. But it was a wonderful day — the company, the method of fishing and the weather all blended to make it an occasion that won't be easily forgotten.

The grass-cutter is out and the first surge of spring growth is being taken off the riverside paths. Early broods of mallard ducklings would slip away unnoticed were it not for their mother attempting to deceive us into believing her wing was broken.

A first litter of mink cubs was discovered on the shelf in the corner of the boathouse — discovered within a day or so of their being born. They were hairless and totally blind and much smaller than most people would believe, in fact almost like a nest of young dormice.

A Couple of Characters

I am beginning to find it hard to define a poacher. We river-keepers lump all offenders under that single heading, yet the occasional hand-liner off the bridge, the sneaker-in at first light and the 'didn't know it was private' fellow have nothing in common with the bloke I met in the pub last week.

We were having our usual 'committee' meeting over a pint, discussing the weather and the state of the river, when this rather nondescript individual with bright red neckerchief and single gold earring asked how the sport was going. Some of my anglers confessed that the wind had been permanently down-stream for a year – or so it had seemed – and that in truth, conditions and bags couldn't be worse. He offered them fish from his van outside.

Up to that point I had taken little interest, but was now suddenly agog with suspicion as to the origin of those trout. When he brought them in they were typical small chalk-stream fellows, and not, as I had expected, rainbows from my stew.

He sold the fish and we asked him if he could get more. After a bit of coaxing and pushing he took us to the lower end of one of my streams and demonstrated poaching in the true sense, or maybe it was fishing in the true sense. Walking close to the bank in ordinary shoes, he removed fish from among tree roots in the water, like you or I would take apples from a tree. With no hesitation or pause to 'tickle' the fish, he produced them with fingers through the gills and hardly a kick. To say I was astounded was putting it mildly. A man like this could empty a fishery and leave a length of river barren. Not knowing my identity, he claimed a working relationship with me. When told who I was he altered the conversation and information to fit another river.

Two of the fish he heaved on to the bank were 3 lb chub, yet he was unaware of the difference between these and trout, and claimed a method of cooking that reduced all fish to a single dish.

Having been in his company for a couple of hours and finding common ground, I got him talking of his fish-taking methods (he objected to its being called poaching). He demonstrated the art of the running noose on a 1½ lb brownie that would have been well beyond me and, perhaps, beyond some of those lads who practise the running noose on the bigger chalk streams. He confessed that salmon, pike and pheasant can all be wired with equal ease. He said that if you go out at night you can shine a light that will dazzle a trout so much that a small landing-net can be slipped beneath it.

I tried it and it's true, but he claimed that the method had the danger of perhaps being spotted by the keeper. When on a serious fish-taking trip he worked with a gang. One would act as a decoy, drawing the keeper's attention and leading him away from the others.

This fascinating character is a country parasite, but I don't mean parasite in any derogatory way. He lives by cropping each portion of the countryside as it becomes ripe – watercress and crayfish, the occasional pearl from the swan mussel, the pick of the orchards a couple of nights before the farmers pick them, and the partridges and pheasants that appear in the game shops on the morning the shooting season starts.

'Because I know you, I will leave you alone,' he promised me, but I believe I shall be on his rota for his yearly visit just as I have been in the past, and that when his battered old van is parked in my area, his crop of trout from my stream will go. It will be an interesting exercise to try and nail him at it.

I have an old gentleman friend who has fished with me for many years and his enthusiasm is such that he infects you with it. Each day is an adventure and every fish he catches a major event. He hooks salmon and the line goes round some obstacle in the water that everybody has evaded for years, yet he manages to get snagged on it. And after hair-raising scrimmages he lands his fish.

He hooks his rod into a tree as he passes underneath it, the bait swings away, falls into the water and is immediately taken by a 26½ lb salmon. An impossible event that actually happened, and could only have happened to this old gentleman.

Last week he hooked a cow. He was facing downstream. The old boy said that something was knocking his prawn and then he heard a splash behind. He presumed it was a salmon jumping, though he did admit that he thought it was rather a large fish! The cow swam downstream into the line, hooked itself and swam on.

You can imagine the scene that followed. Line singing off the reel and the hooked beast mooing its head off in midstream. The old boy said that, given time, he would have landed it had it not clambered up the bank and hared off across the field faster than his reel was meant to work.

He's out again today, fishing the beat below my house, and will get involved with bulls and trees and will tell the tale knowing that we will believe him.

A Rare Visitor

Sometimes, when a monotonous job goes on too long, you welcome the change to a different phase of the year, even though that move means less activity, more sitting, just watching.

Fish moved from hatchery tanks to farms shift the centre of attention to a more isolated environment and to a quieter pattern of life. A twenty-four-hour-a-day vigil with eyes wider open at dawn and dusk – sort of riding shotgun over puddles of water filled to capacity with small defenceless fish, where the balance of Nature is continually having a go at reducing the stocking rate to normal proportions.

Sitting and watching, like being a passenger in a car that travels the same road you have driven over many times before. Time to look and listen and see beyond the roadside hedges. The seagulls, seeing disturbed circles of water breaking, interlocking with never-ending other circles, hover and feed.

From one such trespasser twenty-four corpses were squeezed with the breath of life still working the gills of some of them. And then, of course, the old enemy, 'Nog' the heron, sends the pathfinder over while the main squadron does left-hand circuits way over on the right. Relax, and a thousand fish would disappear down as many throats.

I had a strange visitor who came low across the fields and because the barn owl quarters the area as a welcome guest, I thought it was he. It came in a strange, rather fast-winged flight and dropped in on the side of the pond. I walked forward, wondering, and found the bird had vanished – it was something a conjurer might do.

Spinner, the dog, my constant companion in these days and nights, went past and lunged at a seemingly brown piece of bank and flushed the strangest bird to flight.

In those moments as it gained height, the 12-bore came up, the safety catch was pushed off and my mind ran down a register of possible birds. I pushed the catch to safe as it clicked into the combination of beak, colour and shape which indicated bittern. But there was a difference – the bittern is a heron-sized bird, this was barn-owl size.

A bird book said, 'Little bittern, juvenile night heron and American bittern,' all rare visitors in migrant passage to this country.

A local who is such an expert on these matters that she hops instead of walking thought it most likely to be a little bittern, in which case it was a first sighting in this area for many years. That's as may be, but if the bittern's hunger takes it fishpond-ways again, it will get a fright that will send it scurrying back to its French pals across the water.

Even as I write, the local Ornithological Society is gathering its skirts and assembling in the flight path along the river. What better bird-scarers do I need than that?

In the long hours of watching there are diversions in plenty. I have rod assembled with a spinner and amuse myself in the odd moment by spinning it down through the minnow shoals, past the escaped rainbows feeding on them, and have the wolf-pack of fish chase the flashing spinner up to my feet. They are so quick, those rainbow trout, that the slightest slackening in speed means a wriggling three-quarter-pounder on the end of the line.

The river runs near – no more than a decent cast away – the part that we dredged and where we put a clean gravel run under the bank. Here shoals of barbel spawn in clear water on clean gravel, tails to the weed, head into the current.

A salmon fisherman, all too inexperienced this year in the sight of salmon, fished over one particularly large barbel, going up and down in baits, casts and methods and was too happy at having found a fish to be disillusioned.

It was in this particular piece of water that I watched barbel take the sedge fly as they crawled down the reed to lay their eggs. It was here that a salmon rod hooked and landed a 17 lb barbel that was so full of ripe eggs that they left a patch on the grass, drying in the sun.

The river broadens and an island takes up the slack in the

middle, pushes the two streams of water into a pear-shaped pool, then, joins, narrows and pushes on again. The tail of this stretch always holds a salmon, good year or bad, and this year is no exception. He lies slightly short of midstream from the left-hand bank and obligingly heads and tails at the first sight of fly, bait or spinner. At about the tenth cast he shows his irritation by surging threequarters out of the water in a sideways ballet movement, curved like a bow — the complete gesture of total indifference. Did I say that I had moved from a monotonous job to an even more monotonous occupation? Perhaps I am wrong.

Only one thing spoils the idyllic fisherman's world of trout farm and river and that is a pair of ruddy swans which somehow lost their eggs in the first week of May and blame anyone who walks there for their loss. The hissing and the answering barking created an atmosphere of hate which is a façade on Spinner's part, but sincerely meant by the swans. Though Spinner seems to think it's all a big bluff and that something should be done to show who is boss.

He is saying, 'Come out on the bank,' while the swans want him in the water. I suppose there has to be a snag somewhere.

Part 2: Summer

Vigil at Daybreak

These summer months often mean that I must be out of bed and on the river-bank before daybreak. But don't get me wrong – I don't do it often, nor do I like it. But some of our keener anglers, unable to wait for the opening of the coarse fishing season, will take advantage of these two or three hours when everything is quiet and only the cowmen taking the cows in for the early milking are about to disturb them.

Walking the bank of one of my chalk streams, watching a shoal of very large trout feeding on the spawning minnow, I became aware of a worn patch on the bank and the remnants of a float and bottom fishing tackle hanging from a tree. Hence my early morning jaunt. Concealing myself as near as I could to where the fish were thickest, I settled down to wait for daybreak and my poachers.

As the light filtered in through the trees, a mist descended on the water. Out of this mist flew the silent heron. He glided in and landed on the bank within feet of me. Like an old man out for a walk in a grey raincoat, he stalked the bank anxiously peering into the shallow water, apparently trying to make up his mind whether to get his feet wet or not.

Minnows in their thousands were spawning almost under my feet. Large trout were sending bow-waves across the river as they charged into the eddying shoals. Small chub, dace and grayling which had followed the minnows from deeper water were all in their own ways copying the aggressiveness of the larger trout, while the heron stood motionless in their midst.

Many years ago keepers on chalk streams, whose job it was to shoot and trap herons, used to boil the bird's legs and add the resulting extract to anglers' bait in the belief that something that exuded from them held some attraction for fish.

Across from where I waited a small draw formed the backwater on the river's edge. Here a shoal of large chub found a rival attraction to the minnows. In a slight current coming out of the water meadow, a rope of tadpoles made their way slowly into the main river and into the waiting mouths of the hungry chub. They made no attempt to avoid their end, nor did the chub move sideways to take any that were passing. It was a complete conveyor belt system of feeding. Of the thousands of tadpoles emerging from that draw, I wasn't aware of any getting past that shoal of waiting chub. Which was perhaps as well – all those frogs would have been quite a problem.

In the early light a moorhen shouted an alarm call. This was passed downstream and was taken up by each bird in its own territory. The mute swan croaked its harsh call that is intended to inform everybody on the river that he is not pleased. The heron left the water with one slow beat of its wings, and I began to wonder what it was that was so disturbing the stream.

Without a ripple, with no movement that was perceptible, a small otter drifted down and through the accumulation of fish, past the swans and away round the bend out of sight. There is no doubt as to who is the true head man on the river. Nobody pays that much respect to me when I come downstream.

Two hours after daybreak my poachers arrived with solid glass rods, small fixed-spool reels and a jam-jar full of worms. They were young schoolboys who had found the temptation of this accumulation of large fish too much for them. Of course it is not enough for me to stop them fishing, I must find them another spot where their efforts will not go unrewarded. The grass is starting to grow again and the bank no longer has that beaten-down look about it. But I shall have to keep my eyes on those two youngsters – they have a very capable look.

The French Connection

Sorry to mention my old friend the heron again, but I'm becoming an expert on his life and ways.

If you observe 'Nog' standing in the entrance of the stew on any of his hungry days, watching the food pass beneath him, you'll see that he hasn't got a clue as to his size limitations. Large and small fish – he has a stab at them and puts that lower bill of his through the middle of a large trout that he hasn't a hope of taking from the water.

I've seen fish two or three times his weight pull him off balance and leave him struggling, wings outstretched, on the surface of the water, the serrated edge of his beak holding him in contact with his supposed lunch. One thing he obviously needs is a graded pond where all his meals come in similar sizes.

Grading any sort of fish in numbers has always been a bit of a problem, be they carp, tench or trout. The effort of flipping one this way and one that from a net, is long and painstaking and the end result not all that efficient. We have a riddle arrangement whereby the fish are dropped into a basket, the smaller ones going through, the medium hanging by their gills and the larger having to live out of water longer than they should.

This is not too bad with carp and tench, and the rainbow trout is reasonably hardy, but when you try to to do the same thing with brown trout there are problems. They don't stand up to much knocking about and the slightest damage is infected with a fungus before long.

We have tried screens where you squeeze the fish into a tight group, the small ones running through and leaving the large behind. That's the theory, but they finish hanging from bars like mackerel in a smoking machine.

Someone told me of a new type of grader made in France, so I took out a child's atlas and pin-pointed two inches down towards the middle. It looked a hundred miles the other side of the Channel — no more than a decent afternoon's drive there and back.

I got a catalogue with prices and pictures, even went to see one working across in the next valley. Then loading wife, and part family, into a two-ton pick-up, headed out across Southampton Water to Le Havre and on.

It all looked so simple, but that spot on the map seemed to retreat as we drove. The Continental motorways took some £12 out of my pocket for road tolls, but brought me down to within twenty miles of the Swiss border and almost the same distance from Germany, and to a little town lying like a pebble in the bottom of the gorge where the River Doubs and its canal system run.

The machine was a bundle of polished metal with rods and water going in all directions. A small turbine vibrated through the machine keeping fish on the move, slipping through an appropriate gap and grading them without effort into four preselected sizes. As I watched it work I thought of old Jack back on the fish farm, who, in all weathers during the past two years, has lifted ten tons of fish a week through his potato riddle, with never a complaint.

Loading the machine and paying for it was easy and it left an hour or two to spend before a full day on the road. So what better than to spend it down there on the water's edge with the towering limestone cliffs bending over, casting shadows towards evening.

There was just one angler – non-English-speaking – in many miles of canal path walk, with a longish rod and no reel. There was a vigorous shaking of the head when asked 'What luck?' I couldn't even see what bait he had or even if, in fact, he was fishing! He sat as if he had been told to watch something and hadn't been told to talk.

I sat behind him and watched a barge go through – 250 tonnes of coal from somewhere-up-there to somewhere-down-there. There were a couple of fishing rods on the deck and in answer to my inquiry as to what fish, there was much drawing of pictures, spots on flanks, that could have been anything from a Danubian salmon to a shark.

A friendly fellow with dog companion, a wife to do the driving, a boat half football-pitch length – that to me seemed to be the life. He talked rapidly of fish through the European canal system down to the Mediterranean. He talked so fast that every tenth word was understood and this made sense of the conversation. All this while his dog growled defiance at any thought of my intruding on the deck.

A lady worked the lock, pulled the heavy wheels, wound the spanners and fed her miserable thin dogs on a loaf of bread and a bucket of water from the river – the sort of situation which the RSPCA and the Sunday newspapers would have lived on for a week in this country. Between trips her barge dogs were kept in a hovel beneath the lock-keeper's cottage, ribs showing and hygiene non-existent. For the price of ten francs I bought six tins of dog meat and borrowed a tin-opener in the local town. I managed to persuade two local lads, again of the non-English-speaking variety, to come with me, and at the risk of being mauled, fed the poor brutes. We raised a glimmer in the eyes of the angler as he pulled a similar tin from his pocket and showed what bait he had been using.

The trip home was uneventful. There were some anglers on the Seine in Paris, but as the traffic was going the wrong way, it was difficult to watch and drive at the same time. All parking spaces had been occupied for years.

They let me on the boat at Le Havre with the signing of a few forms but had no intention of letting me out of Customs at Southampton without Customs declarations that would have taken a genius to fill in. Having been in maximum security for hours and with little else to do before the next boat, they took an interest in the machine and suddenly they were anglers, not just Customs men.

We got talking and I found that they would appreciate an occasional day's fishing or a box of trout maybe, if we came that way.

I was on the road within minutes, they with my telephone number, me with a fistful of forms to fill in at my leisure, and a short half-hour from my bed.

That spot in France was a thousand miles on the clock when it had looked only a few hours away.

Strange Happenings

Why is it that some people have strange things happen to them? One of my rods, Mr Dick Smith of Southall, a good fisherman, has more than his share of strange happenings. Recently he and I were fishing a deep hole on the edge of an island, swinging a heavy Devon behind an ounce and a half of lead. As often happens when the water is cold and you are trying to keep a bait as near the bottom as possible, we hooked into something that was immovable. No amount of strain on the line would move it, it was impossible to get below the obstruction and put strain on from that direction, so we looked around for something to use as an 'otter'.

A half-bottle of beer was hurriedly drunk. A loop of string was tied securely to the bottle's neck and then round the line, and the bottle was slid off into the depths, down, we hoped, to the snagged bait, the current pulling the bottle in the reverse direction to the rod. Whether it was successful or not we shall never know, for no sooner did the bottle disappear into the depths than the line started to sing off the reel with the pull of a good fish.

I don't think a salmon has ever before had to fight for its life with a beer bottle hanging alongside it!

Every time the gaff was brought out, thinking the fish was beat, that bottle would bang into its side like a jockey's whip and off would go the fish.

Eventually he tired sufficiently to be grassed, surely the craziest bit of salmon fishing this river has seen for many a day. Its weight was 29 lb – our biggest fish of the year so far, and, I think, the unluckiest.

The approach of summer and the water not striking too cold, I was tempted to have my first swim of the year.

For some time now I have been intrigued with one of my salmon lies. This is on a slight bend in the river with no apparent feature showing on the surface to make it attractive to fish. And yet, consistently over the years, early salmon show there and are caught there. It is a good swim for coarse fish – not chub or roach, but dace and grayling find it most attractive. The surface area is always dimpled with rising trout and yet it is on a piece of river showing nothing of what is hidden beneath the surface.

Putting on my wet-suit, a full bottle of air on my back, and with two of my anglers holding the boat steady, I slipped over the side some thirty yards upstream.

I was mistaken about the water. As it squeezed in through the cracks in the suit and filled up my rubber socks, I had the impression that it was mid-winter and that the sun had not had time to warm it. Through ten feet of water I allowed the current to push me along an almost weed-clear bed. This started to rise, then dipped sharply into quite a deep hole. At the bottom of the hole a powerful spring bubbled out of the strata, a spring so powerful that it was almost impossible to hold my position at the centre of it.

Millions of gallons of water were being forced out of the chalk hills above the river. Immediately behind the spring the bed of the river formed a narrow valley of bright clean gravel, with all the signs of having been freshly disturbed by the tail of the resting salmon.

The reason for the popularity of this spot was clear: fish entering the river from the sea in early spring, found this warmer water, liked it, and stayed there.

First-day Carping

The early morning of 16 June arrives with the meadows shrouded in almost a fog. The hour is not long after 3 a.m., and, like the cartoons in the angling papers, humped figures on the bank wait for first light and a first glimpse of a float.

Somebody persuaded me to cross the line between the Wessex and the Thames Water Authorities, leave my river for others on the opening day of the coarse season, and fish for carp in an obscure muddy hole surrounded by reed and with an apparent depth of six inches of water two or three rod-lengths out. The only carp I have caught came from a gravel pit that was being filled in and where the fish were so compressed that anything which fell into the water was food.

This was different. I was told to seek a deep corner, to find a spot where the Canadian weed overlapped by lily pads didn't fill the water, and watch in that warm morning air for signs of feeding fish. I was issued with a bagful of golf balls consisting of some secret mix that stuck to the fingers like sago pudding and put a smear down the front of my jersey that, as it dried later, became armour plating that would have stopped a bullet. A 13 ft salmon rod and 10 lb line completed the outfit.

I found the right pitch and fished. Somebody, full of advice, pinched a piece of silver paper on to the loose line between the reel and first rod ring, so instead of being able to watch the countryside around me gradually unveil, I watched the chocolate-smeared silver bite recorder as intently as was deemed necessary. That is, for the first hour, or was it a week?

When the sun was two feet above the horizon, the day already well advanced, flask of coffee disposed of and a half-bottle of Scotch showing down the first inch of the label, the time was still only 6 a.m.

Already the world of animals and birds had been up, breakfasted, cleaned, washed and settled down for a mid-morning siesta before the day could start.

A moorhen chivvying in the sedge marked the passage of something that walked and attracted the attention of a couple of swans and a single scruffy cygnet, so that they all came and peered intently.

Mallard duck came out of the rush, peering backwards so that I began to wonder what strange animal had attracted the eyes focused no more than a yard or so to my right. Whatever it was must have been gazing with the same intense feeling at me.

The silver paper bobbed and the line tightened – then slackened again and, as if at a tennis match, my eyes went from the line to a renewed rustling on my right. The inquisitive swans stared right through me, then the one to my left barracked with that unmelodious croak which gives the mute swan its name instead of trying to find a name for the noise it makes.

The silver paper jumped again, the rod bent and I tightened. Whatever it was down there in the water did a tango on the spot and festooned the line with weed so that it vanished into a cone of dark green moving rubbish.

I shouted for my guide and companion who came bustling up with eyes like organ stops and babbled a tale of some animal that had passed close behind him with the sound of at least a herd of steers. I pointed to the bent rod and the disguised lump trying to move below the surface and had a gallant offer from him to wade out and see if he could dislodge whatever it was. Apparently it was a good carp of 8 or 9 lb, or so he said.

The shallow appearance of the water over and above the weed, however, was a total lie – a trap to snare the unwary, for after a single step out from the bank, gently prodding in front of him, my guide vanished. His glorious fly-arrayed hat, with mounted 'hedge sparrows' fore and aft, floated until a hand came up and grabbed it and placed it back on the balding head that appeared alongside.

He was wet, so he went on, while I claimed I only had a few feet of line out, which was an untruth if ever there was one. He followed the line for more than twenty yards and brought up an empty hook with more weed than appeared possible from the area. I still say the fish was 8 or 9 lb, perhaps more, and the landlord of the pub we sat outside until they opened at ten in the morning confirmed the story of such monsters.

I went back home to the Avon before lunch to an opening day as sad as any. Very few dace and lots of trout, when dace were the prime target. A 6 lb barbel to someone angling for salmon and a couple of 4 lb out-of-condition chub when early morning roach were needed.

The day was brightened by our young Water Resources biologists putting lots of little coloured cubes in a regular pattern across the eel trap outfall, miniature housing blocks for the small citizens of the river.

The test is to see if they prefer a particular colour, to see if they avoid one, or if a red sitting-room for shrimps is everything they have ever wished for.

Done to a Turn

Mid-July and everything has slowed down. The volume of water flowing downstream is but a trickle compared to the power and force of early spring. Sedges, rushes and riverweed have all reached the end of their growth and have but a short life into the autumn.

Small summer salmon continue to find their way upstream in ones and twos, running over the shallows with their backs out of the water, only the momentum of their travel keeping them upright. Sea-trout that haven't the patience to wait in the river for their eggs to mature now start to come in from the sea in increasing numbers.

These short, deep, exciting fish fight, pound for pound, better than any other that swims in our waters. I look forward to August rain when the larger 10 to 15-pounders push their way into the small forest streams and seize the offered bait with the same eagerness with which, a few hours before, they chased the whitebait of the estuary.

This eagerness is short-lived. Within hours of entering fresh water they become secretive and selective in their habits. In fact, once they get inland a little way, they seem to vanish, although the pools that hide them are no larger than bath-tubs.

The first eels feel the need to go downstream. Not many – about half a dozen a night during the July dark – they average, in these early eeling days, about 1½ lb, with an occasional 3 to 4-pounder.

These eels, given plenty of room in the storage tank, keep well. They stay happy for a month or so until I can accumulate enough to send a box into the market.

The only difficulty in storing them is that they shrink in numbers once my anglers get wind that there are a few about.

This period of high summer has not been without incident on the salmon fishing front. One of my salmon fishermen fished from early in the year with very little success. He hooked and lost each fish he came across. Gradually his face became longer and longer until it was impossible for me to cheer him up.

On his allocated day earlier this month he started fishing at 9.30 in the morning. With his second cast he found himself securely attached to a fish straight from the sea. After a hard fight it was grassed, weighed at 17 lb, wrapped in a polythene bag and put in the boot of his car. As time went on, the sun climbed higher and the day developed into one of those real scorchers that lifted the temperature into the high seventies. Another fish was hooked and lost and the warming water caused several stale fish to move uneasily in their holts, encouraging my fisherman to carry on through the hot part of the day.

At six o'clock in the evening, his rods were broken down and the car driven the ten miles or so home. There the fish was disturbed for the first time since it had been caught in the morning. It was grasped by the tail and lifted out – and imagine the consternation of the angler when the fish fell, leaving the tail in his hand.

I was phoned and, with disease in mind, the River Authority was also informed. They sensed the urgency and sent their biologist post-haste to view and take his samples from the fish. The result of his inquiries was not long in coming – the fish was cooked to a turn. All it needed was some lettuce and a bit of salad cream.

That angler hasn't fished again. He says: 'Enough. I'll wait for next season and make a fresh start.'

The Hackle Hunters

In my youth when, to me fly-fishing was the most important thing in the world, I collected the capes of every cockerel that I could get my hands on. No farmyard rooster was safe in the area that I lived in. I tied my own flies and kept an assortment of people supplied as well.

Then, as the years dribbled away, anglers started to give me a few and others who passed on left me fly-boxes stuffed with them. So gradually I stopped tying my own, except for that one pattern which, to me, is the most useful of all flies, the Lunns

Particular. This fly has a pair of fine hackle points tied in with the hackle proper. It is an exquisite creation which can represent any of the olives that hatch from our streams.

The hackle points are a delicate shade of blue, and though they can be obtained in the dyed form, the true cockerel hackles of that colour are to be preferred. But they are extremely rare.

A few miles from my cottage there lives a lady whose garden and farmyard are inhabited by a motley collection of inbred bantams. I have coveted from a distance one of the elder statesmen of these bantams for some years. The blue of his neck feathers, plus his great age, made his cape a most desired thing. The lady would not consider selling him, but gave a half-hearted promise that when he passed on, I could have the corpse.

This is blue-winged olive time and Lunns Particular time. In desperate need for just a few of those fine hackle points, the local doctor – whose patient the lady was – and I, managed to persuade her to let us have just a few of the feathers from the bird. He was caught after a short scuffle and an undignified dive by the doctor. With great precision three or four dozen of the finer points were plucked from the neck and the cockerel was then released to join his wives.

But my friend and I are the losers. Within twenty-four hours of this incident the aged bird passed away. With this attack on his person so fresh in her mind, the lady now refuses to hand over the body. More than this, she threatens to change her doctor and her farm gate has suddenly sprouted a large padlock.

My coarse anglers, incensed by the salmon anglers' success with the barbel, have been laying siege in the barbel swims. They have trotted, legered with swim-feeders, and, as a last resort, copied the salmon angler in trundling a small crayfish through the gravelly run. But the big fellow they all seek seems to have learned his lesson and is, at the moment, keeping his mouth shut.

A group of anglers in conversation at our local fishy pub, The Bull at Downton, were on common ground when talking of a particularly good pool that holds large salmon, barbel and almost everything else that swims in the river. A bottom fisherman said he hooked a large barbel on some legered cheese which ran out every inch of his 120-yard line of 8 lb breaking strain, severing it at the reel, while still going downstream like an express train.

My salmon angler, fresh from some success in the same pool, said he hooked a 21 lb salmon on a small boiled crayfish in the same swim. This fish also bolted downstream and was eventually landed 200 yards lower down.

The point under discussion for the rest of the evening was why should the salmon angler follow his fish downstream as a matter of course, while the barbel man saw no reason why he should lift his backside off his stool.

Military Manoeuvres

During the last war, this estate was the headquarters of an American Army group. The home of my employer harboured its officers and the grounds and woods housed the other ranks. Consequently, the estate's waters were used in various ways, some legal, some not. Nets from the tennis courts were weighted and pulled down the small feeder streams while various substances that made fishing with the rod and line completely out of date were dipped in the river.

Stew-ponds had to be guarded night and day to ensure that anything survived and one asset was that these fish grew magnificently on the minced-up remnants from the cookhouse.

The keeper of those days should have died young but in fact it gave him a fund of stories that carried him beyond his allotted years. He was fortunate that the American general in charge later began to take an interest in angling. This gradually developed, with a bit of crafty prompting from the estate, into a great passion. The keeper's job suddenly became very easy: Service police were allocated as under-keepers – and such under-keepers! They patrolled with carbines – a bullet permanently up the spout.

Junior officers were encouraged to fly-fish the chalk streams, while other ranks were allocated the mixed fishery or the main river. Local people donated tackle of all sorts so that gradually the whole camp became fishing-mad.

So from a country rich in fisheries, many men came to this piece of England to start on a pastime that would persist for the rest of their lives. In the last few years some of them have returned to look again and perhaps relive a few hours from their youth.

Such a man, a junior officer during the war, now a very high-ranking general with NATO, recently came to fish.

As we walked the water he talked of casting his fly to a fish, of catching it, and having it served for his dinner in the mess. He talked of his disappointment over its texture and taste. Only later, when he caught and ate his first trout, did he discover that the other fish had been a chub.

In his native country this man is a respected and noted angler, so the return to the start of his angling life was a mixture of nostalgia and eagerness to get on the water. Alas, something must have altered over the years. It couldn't have been the river. His whole beat, as he remembered it, now proved too far to walk in a morning and the cast into the shadow of a stone bridge produced only yards of fly-line round the back of his neck and shoulders.

The day was hot, the water clear and not a ripple of any sort disturbed the glass-like surface. The only chance there was of getting a fish was to move upstream into the broken water of the weir. Here we were fortunate – a single fish out on the far side was persistently dimpling the surface, taking the tiny ceanis (the Fisherman's Curse) one after the other.

I pointed this fish out, saying that I thought it was too far for him to cast. 'Not at all, I can manage that,' my American general assured me. As I said, the day was bright, the car with drinks was near, this was as good a spot as any to spend an hour or so.

So I encouraged him through the day while he tried what was obviously, to me at least, beyond him. Every time he appeared to flag a little I would put in a 'Nearly, that time, sir.' He would then renew his efforts while I reached again for my glass.

Eventually a cast somehow or other went right, the fast water through the middle delayed its pull on the line so that the fly floated for that fraction of a second that was needed.

A nose came out, the fly was sucked in, and you could almost predict that trout's thoughts. 'Not what I am feeding on but an acceptable change in the day's diet,' for surely no trout had ever seen a bright red-bodied fly with purple wings on this river for many years.

Beauty in a fish is something only anglers see. This 2½ lb brownie was spotted three-quarters of the way down his depth with big thumb-nail size brown spots. Its fins had that rim of red that trout in perfect condition sometimes have.

It was the fish to catch on a one-fish day.

The 'Drowner' Departs

When the final roll call of those who have done the most for angling is called, I don't suppose for one moment that Jack Earney will feature on it.

There'll be famous names in writing who have told the world what they have done and are doing, while others will hover around the perimeter and hope to be included.

Jack Earney will wander his own quiet way and in the final count will probably head the field. He was a 'drowner' by profession, as his family were before him – uncles, nephews etc. He worked in the dark of winter's mornings pulling back the river edges so that the width of the stream remained the same.

More than that, on the obscure carriers and drawings, he cut out the unneeded and left the flowering so that not only did those waterways stay alive to fish, but were gardened. Hundreds of acres, criss-crossed by water, fashioned into a water garden in a way that nobody before or since has done.

He was a countryman in the true sense of the word, a naturalist who knew nothing yet knew everything, who could paint a picture in words with the expertise of long practice yet hid the fact that he couldn't write. He had his own names for every animal and bird because at no time had he been in contact with the written description and names of his water-meadow friends. He would pull a piece of hedge to one side and show me where the 'bird mouse' had nested, not caring for the more familiar name of Long-tailed Tit.

When the hunts came through for the otter, he would send them in every direction but where his friends were lying up.

He joined me on the river a few short years ago and took his story-telling to a wider audience of half a dozen young river-keepers. He would tell of the injured animal crawling into a hole either to recover or die, and Jack, in the true sense of the countryman, followed the same line in the last months of his life.

It was obvious from his attitude, the gradual slowing down of his work-rate, that all was not right. A man as lean as he, with no surplus weight, had only to lose a pound to look emaciated.

He still swung his scythe along the river banks, his eyes still not needing assistance from spectacles, but now he worked less and leaned more, 'till the leaning filled a large part of the day.

He worked his end to within a day or so. He asked for his three weeks' holiday in one piece, went home and moved into his chair by the sitting-room window and in ten days was gone. He crawled into his own personal corner and, like the words of Johnnie Mercer, 'We lost him to a summer wind.'

Fifty-three years without a break, each and every day, through every weekend he walked the river. All that collected knowledge lost, and with it, so many deep and understanding friendships.

Looking back

'Fishing for sale' – it's an advertisement that always draws my attention. This one was in one of those glossy magazines that gives you all the hunting, fishing and shooting news and very little else.

The agent's story of several miles of fishing, keeper's cottage and grand lodge glowed with sales ploy. So much so that I was on to the photographs before I realized that this was the beat on the Itchen where I first changed to the river from game-keepering.

I loved the piece about the charming keeper's cottage on the water's edge – no mention in the advert of the rising damp that made the wallpaper stand two inches from the wall, or the roar of the river when in flood that made it impossible to hold a conversation in any voice below a shout. But then, in compensation, there was the soft whisper from the water when the summer willow trailed its leaves in that silver river.

As a gamekeeper keen on fish and rivers – as distinct from being a keen angler – I made the shift into that waterside cottage and moved into a part of fishery ownership that was a thing. My new employer, then in his eighties, was surrounded by friends who belonged to those same vintage years. The river, some five miles of it, was kept in private ownership and restricted to these few aged and highly privileged people.

Our season never started before the Mayfly was on the water. Early hatches of Olives and Iron Blues were ignored as they didn't bring the really big fellows on to surface feed, but once the season did start it was in its way unique.

A car to the station in the morning, chauffeur dressed to the eyes, black polished leggings and all, escorting rheumaticky guests and their tackle to a point in the grounds outside the fishing-room where I would go through the ceremony of greeting and assembling their tackle.

One of these old boys – a High Court judge – would return all his catch each day to the water, then when standing over his first drink in the evening, would tell the biggest whoppers to his host, exaggerating his catch, while I would be required to nod my head in agreement.

Another old gentleman was so tottery on his limbs that he refused to cross any single-plank bridge. He would wade up to his waist through the side-streams and dry out during the day and call this a safer way of walking the bank.

This same angler knocked at my cottage door one lunchtime and, discovering that I was eating, said he would wait in the sunshine until I was finished. That gentleman had hooked a 4 lb trout and, being unable to land it, had walked half a mile or so for my help and was then willing to wait while I finished my meal.

One friend I had in those days, who alas, like the rest has now gone, was Sir Alfred Herbert, that colossus of the machine-tool world. He would glide up to my cottage in his limousine and remain seated until the chauffeur and I had everything prepared for his leisurely parade up the water, he leading, his entourage like porters, following in single file.

Just after his ninetieth birthday, Sir Alfred's wife moved a very large trout to an artificial Mayfly, but she was unfortunate enough to hook the sedge near the fish, and in pulling her line loose, put the fish down for the day.

On the following day Sir Alfred tried for the fish and also hooked the sedge, but not being caught by the mistakes of his

wife, he borrowed another rod, cast again, hooked and landed a 6 lb 1 oz trout, which on a dry fly is something of an achievement.

To quote Sir Alfred: 'It was worth living to ninety to do that.'

It is hardly believable that at this sale of water someone will buy it and be able to afford to restrict its use as in its past, for I hear through the grapevine that it has a poacher problem which even surpasses the two hundred I had in my first year.

The only way to get over that sort of thing is to fill the water with legitimate anglers and leave little room for the rest.

The Poaching Habit

The poaching season seems to have arrived. Almost every time I take a quick look round the water I find cars with bits of tackle on the back seat or under the dash, a sure sign that someone has wandered off with the rest of their gear on a quiet look round for a fishy spot.

I found such a car the other day with the usual bits and pieces lying around, so in the slow lumbering gallop that is my style nowadays, I took myself off downstream, dark thoughts brooding in my mind towards anyone that I might find. Yet after an hour's searching all I could find was a couple of nuns picnicking under a riverside willow. After passing them several times I had to ask them: 'Was the car theirs?' Yes it was, and the tackle on the back seat, that belonged to young students at a school where they taught. What could be more straightforward than that? A sweet smile for me and they continued with their feet-in-the-water meal.

Since then I have had further thoughts. Are the town poachers getting as crafty as their country cousins? If that pair in the black habits come back again, a little watching might be in order.

On a river such as this that caters for the visiting angler it would be easy to ignore the local ones and thereby get the villagers poaching left, right and centre.

To fill the river with the well-off and to price the fishing rights out of the pockets of the not so well-off would be the height of folly. But then I learned this the hard way when I first came to this estate.

Our local yokels used to get up to all sorts of dodges, especially the younger ones. Angling to these village boys is not the organized day out it is to the town lad.

With more time on their hands, they use the river as the town boys would use the street corner. Night-lines with rows of codling hooks with any fish that swims as their target, eel traps built from sacks and bicycle wheels that used to supply — and may still do — many an eel for a village family.

They build boats out of oil drums and my weir-boards and search the little-used backwaters for extra large fish. With face mask and snorkel they will spend a summer chasing one particular fish, going back time and again as the mood gets into them.

I try to organize them by letting them fish a piece of water that is theirs alone, lending them a proper boat to save oily waste getting on the water. Yet they still creep a little on the permit, always finding it better on the other side of the fence.

I wouldn't have them any other way for they grow up understanding what the countryside is all about.

One old gent along the river gave a lot of trouble for some years. He would wander the river bank in the early spring, a cross between a heron and an otter, all eyes and a feeling for the tremors and warnings that he had been brought up to understand.

He would search until he found a carrion crow's nest in the making. Once he found this he knew he could have three months of well-guarded sport. Equipped for his day's activities he would move into a selected swim, the crow slipping off her nest at his approach, keeping the cover of the nesting tree between them.

The cock carrion then takes a hand in the nest-protection game, sitting himself on a sentinel tree. This tree, commanding views in all directions, is used to keep an eye on the intruder and at the same time watch the rest of the countryside for further activity in its area.

It is a well-known fact that the crow can spot a man with gun or dog almost as soon as he leaves his keeper's cottage. And that old poacher could read the bird like a book.

The crow would ignore village children and the cowman taking in the herd for afternoon milking, but at the approach of a keeper it would take a safe route out of the territory, closely followed by the old gent and his day's catch. He was impossible to creep up on in these circumstances so I compromised by finding him a small piece of water that was his alone.

An Angler's Dream

Many keen anglers dream of retiring to the country, there to look after a length of river or a lake, to trim the grass, cut the weed and generally make a labour out of looking after great, fat, lazy fish. But the dream and reality are so far apart that few achieve it.

One who did came to me in the first place as a sergeant in the Royal Marines, and after scrounging a day or two on my carriers he became deeply interested in the day-to-day goings-on at the fishery.

When he was about to retire on pension, he managed to persuade his officers that the last month of his Service life would be well spent helping me with my work. In that month we worked a little, but spent most of our time visiting various colleagues on other fisheries, mixed and pure trout. We saw rivers where under-keepers worked a 70-hour week in conditions that would have caused a walk-out in any other industry. We also visited keepers with no interest in fish whatsoever, and as a consequence lacked the push to make a success of the job.

The sergeant was not put off by anything he saw, so we let it be known along the river valleys that I knew of a good man who wanted a job and soon we got him settled on a pure trout stream in the head-waters of one of our chalk streams.

In the three years that have passed since then, he could have been forgiven, I think, had he occasionally taken up his coarse tackle and practised among the willing trout in his weir pools, but quite the contrary. When he discovered a shoal of three roach in his upper water he guarded them with the same pride of possession that he gave his trout.

Small inlets have been carved into the river bank, each one carefully selected for its position in gravelly shallows. Into these, safe from larger fish, trout fry assemble out of the major current.

Those enemies of all well-kept trout streams — mud and silt — he has tackled in a way that is both ingenious and effective.

Across the stream he moors a telegraph pole, pegged into the bank at both ends on strong chains. From the pole to the bed of the river, corrugated iron sheeting funnels fast-moving water into the mud.

It is only a matter of minutes' work each day to move the sheeting so as to clear a given width of river, then a few more minutes' work to move the pole on to the next muddy spot. He found a small trickle of spring water making the river bank soggy. This was channelled and bridged and then thousands of trout eggs were hatched in what once had been a bog.

A derelict eel trap has been rebuilt and every migrating eel that tries to slip away in the night is trapped and sold to add to the revenue of the river.

The river-banks have the appearance of being mown with a push-mower, the riverside herbage is trimmed to a uniform height along both sides of this mile or so of fishing. Hundreds of tons of chalk and earth have been carted to firm the banks and narrow the water channel where the river was too wide to keep itself clean.

River-borne flies are encouraged to lay their eggs on the safety of boards floating well out of the way of any eel looking for a quick snack.

Jim's piece of river, that was once only in his dreams, is now undoubtedly the show-piece of the South of England, and still he works and his mind runs ahead with further projects. He plans to do away with all the old wooden bridges that hold up the cut weed on their centre pillars.

Single span with steel girders is now apparently the thing. A rainbow trout pool is still in his mind, and I have no doubt that that too will soon be a fact.

Too often a change of job turns a little sour and dreams don't turn out quite as they should, but here is a man who in a few short years is now showing us longer-established keepers the way it should be done.

A Star Performer

This week has been a mixture of comedy and controversy. We had Eric Morecambe down for a day, and if you have ever fished with a comedian of his rank, you will understand that he takes his studio along with him – hysterics that last you through your fishing-time and would cost you a fortune if you had to pay for them!

We fished through the deep water below Salisbury, throwing a spinner into the accessible corners, catching a few small pike and a chub that mistook the Mepp for a fleeing minnow. Then towards evening we changed to wet fly through the fast shallows.

There was a sort of uneasy quiet to the end of the day, a dark thunderstorm coming down the chalk stream from the right and, as often happens in this sort of evening, a hatch of fly from the head of the broken water.

It started slowly with one or two fish splashily rising and some sort of signal that went downstream to warn fish of what was likely to happen.

Furrow marks started to move up as large trout took their place at the table. A slight breeze and a few large drops of rain from the moving thunderstorm, rumbles in the distance and a hurried glance at any metal parts in our tackle.

Now I'm not going to say that Eric Morecambe is a good fisherman, or even that he is a lousy fisherman, but somewhere between the two he makes up for his deficiences with the amount of labour and effort he puts in against the fish. Without moving from one set position, he cast one of those monstrosities that look like a hedge-sparrow – a bundle, of white wool stuck to a large hook leaded to sink fast. It was taken by a 4 lb rainbow that went in all directions, even making a half-hearted attempt to climb the river-bank into the nettles and overhanging brambles.

Netted and in the bag, it was joined by a six-pounder twenty minutes later, which by my way of thinking, was good enough to call it a day.

The trout were not as plentiful as one might have thought from this success, however, for most of the fish that were bulging in the various ripples were chub, dace and a cross-section of varied-sizes of splashy grayling.

While we were talking and watching the thunderstorm move away downstream, we thought that one of the fish taking fly some distance away in the quieter, slacker water of the tail was lifting and moving more water than a small fish would do. Five or six minutes later we got below him and tossed our woollie sparrow into the window of his vision and frightened him into a fit of the sulks.

We sat and drank some peat-coloured water from Scotland with the addition of alcohol, and waited until he came out and started to take the hatching BWO again. A change of cast to the 4x and of fly to a Lunn's Particular – small blue wings spread-eagled in a haze of fine Jungle Cock hackle, a body ribbed and three carefully chosen cock pheasant fibres as whiskers.

We floated it over his nose and the fight was on. Eight pounds of trout that went like a steam engine in every possible combination of fishing tricks that when landed had us both more excited than our professional experience should have allowed.

I photographed the fish, of course, lying on paper bearing a portrait of another comic-cum-singer – a gentleman whose name I daren't mention in case he adds my name to his anti-Eric Morecambe jokes!

The controversy of the week occurred in one of our local hotels where anglers with a more discerning eye than the general run of tourists suggested that the name 'salmon trout' didn't belong to the fish that was on the cold buffet table and being offered for lunch.

It had been cooked by a bloke in a big, white, tall hat, who in local hotels is politely called 'chef', which I think in this case was near enough to being true as to be not worth disputing.

The fish weighed 12 lb and when cooked, and the skin folded back, was served in the restaurant as salmon trout. It had a little card stuck into the flesh just below the dorsal quoting the price of a portion, and because it was within the scope of most people's holiday pocket, was a popular choice.

I like to do my little bits of market research so I talked to waiters and customers with a mini-questionnaire. 'Did you enjoy it?' Which everyone seemed to. 'Did you think it was Atlantic salmon or Pacific salmon?' Giving them choice of which neither was true.

The fish was in fact one of my normal rainbow trout fed on 60 per cent of protein instead of the much lower normal trout diet. It had put curds between the flakes of flesh and added a shoulder of muscle to the rather short fish for its length and weight. Then, with a bit of jiggery-pokery, the flesh was made to resemble that of a spring salmon by the inclusion of a vegetable dye.

I firmly believe that a lot of taste appreciation is in the eye of the beholder and if a name is given and the looks agree with the name, then very few people argue about it.

The Trade Descriptions Act is being nudged just a little for while there may be some base steelhead salmon trout strain in the modern rainbow trout, they have been bred and interbred through Kamloops, Shasta, Kern River and goodness knows what else, until the jam-pot of a mixture can be called just about what you like and yet still have some resemblance to truth.

I sent a load of these so-called salmon trout into a fishery – short, deep, fat, silver fish that looked more like sea trout fresh into the river. I compared them with sea trout from the lower end of the River Avon. I even mentally compared the maggot-caught fish from this river with the fighting qualities of the mixed-up rainbow trout.

I came to the conclusion that taste, fightability and appearance were all about equal and if implanted into rivers cut off from the sea, either by material barrier or pollution, they would give just as good an account of themselves as fresh-run salmon – weight for weight – and be a darned sight cheaper in the overall costing as against salmon hatcheries, gillies and the impedimenta of travelling to Scotland and back.

A Horror Story

My eel trap, though producing very few eels at the moment, is still providing its annual spectacular. The river flow has decreased to a very low summer level. Weed shows above the surface where normally it should be flattened to the bed by the pace of the current. Everywhere hatches are being closed and weirs boarded up; in fact everything possible is being done to keep the river at a decent level.

What little water there is can be taken easily by the eel-trap hatches, making the fast water below the trap the only well-oxygenated stretch of stream available to the fish. There they accumulate to grab what food they can.

The July-August grilse, still managing to find a way round the various turbines of the lower river, has his way barred by the eel-trap slats. He, being less mature than the spring and summer salmon, finds a resting-place in the most turbulent of water, accumulating friends from the sea trout as they too work their way upstream.

Shoals of small trout, as silvery as a sixpence, flash in the water as they take the spawning minnow, for while fish that gather below the trap need this type of water, so does the minnow to lay its eggs and reproduce.

Barbel, bigger – or so they seem – than any we have ever caught, lie in close-packed ranks, then, like a living carpet, surge forward as the minnow shoals form and eddy, their mouths working as they sort out eggs from gravel. Then there is a small movement backwards as the debris is rejected.

The real aquarium look comes when the water is turned off. Chub seem to materialize from nowhere. They mill around investigating the still water that they suddenly find themselves in.

Showing a complete loss of direction, they join with the dace moving round the confines of the run, until a fish in the procession finds the main river by accident. Then out they go into it to take up fresh positions in the altered water flow.

There is a stale very red cock salmon who nightly journeys from some secret holt to the pool below the eel trap, then, when the water is turned off, joins the tail of the dace procession and slips back to the river. This last fortnight he has become a regular feature among the fishy gallery. I get the feeling that at this stage of his life, with the autumn before him and spawning due in December, he is using too much of his stored-up energy with this nightly roaming around.

With the growth of popularity of aquariums and rapid transport, all sorts of fishes find their way from river to river. In the packed ranks below the eel trap we have a single tench that somehow survives the years, and last week we almost had a catfish! One of my rods legering a bunch of worms among the milling fish had a run that tore some twenty yards of line from the reel, then nothing. He reeled in and discovered his line had broken just above the hook. He suspected salmon, but wasn't too sure.

He baited up again and cast into the same spot and two chub and a trout later the same thing happened, the line breaking between the lead and the hook. Not to be outdone by any fish he tied on his hook with a strong single-strand wire pike trace and cast again into the identical spot. And again came the thump and the short powerful run of a good fish. He rang me at my home in absolute panic. 'Somebody,' he said, 'has put catfish into the river. At least, I think they are catfish.'

When I arrived at the fishing site he was the centre of a small group of anglers gathered at the edge of the eel trap staring into the water. The angler hadn't bothered to land the fish. He had left it suspended on his tackle as far out of his reach as he could get it. Its colour was a bluish-green, merging with an orange colour showing on its belly every time it twisted in the water.

Holding it on a tight line, I vow I have never seen such a horror in my life. It was obviously no catfish. In fact it was something that I had never seen before. We finally decided, with help from a keeper downstream, that this was a sea lamprey.

This keeper reminded me that legend claims that King John died from eating a surfeit of lamprey and asked if we were going to eat it.

Eat it? It was such an ugly brute that we didn't dare land it. Later I learned that these 18-inch to 24-inch fish come into the river to spawn, and need, like the minnow, fast gravelly runs to secure their eggs.

The Purist Approach

Letting fishing has quite a few snags. Good tenants are difficult to find and members to fit in with happy syndicates are scarce. I was called into the office and informed by the Estate that a certain farm about ten miles from the centre of the estate was going to be put up for sale. As this included about one mile of chalk-stream fishing, I was being brought in to discuss some of the details of the sale.

The fishing to be sold is let to a gentleman who trims his own banks and generally looks after it himself. He is a dry-fly purist and a naturalist of some standing. When the water was first let to him some years ago I walked him round and pointed out the various pools, fast runs and dark corners. This was a pretty little stream, rising from a series of artesian springs that have never been known to run dry.

It had a good rate of fall over its entire length, its bed was clean and the banks firm. All in all, one of those streams that one dreams of retiring to. There is a perpetual haze of surface feed and a constant dribble of freshwater shrimp. It is the sort of place where you can kneel and catch a half-pound trout from among a herd of Friesian cattle standing cooling in the clear water. Over recent years I haven't interfered. Our tenant has fished happily and I have met him at the social occasions that I organize to draw our various tenants and syndicate members together. Now I had to go and view this water afresh, and view it as would a potential buyer. What a surprise this stream gave us.

Small bushes that had once given shade had now grown out and covered the water. Rushes that clad the banks now marched into midstream. Little hatch-pools that had had small clumps of bramble in one corner were now covered in so completely as to be almost impossible to fish.

The fast gravelly runs had an accumulation of the debris of years of high water. The stream that had once been the delight of a previous tenant now had the appearance of a derelict swamp.

By arrangement I met the rent-payer on the bank with his rod and I asked him how it was that each time I had met him his enthusiasm for this fishing had seemed so great and yet he had allowed it to deteriorate into its present state. My friend disclaimed any deterioration. To him the stream hadn't altered.

He walked a few yards, bent his knee and with a sideways flick of his small brook rod he expertly cast a fly into a dark shadow under the alders. A fish of a pound rose and took his fly, careered downstream into a tunnel of scrub and overhanging trees, was neatly played into the bank, through the flag iris and netted.

At an overgrown hatch-pool the fly was put on the small piece of tail-water showing from under the bramble. A fish rose and rushed upstream to the head of the pool. With his rod-tip poked under the surface our tenant played another fish out of the gloom into the bank. Where the stream had narrowed, the water ran fast and deep and from this reed-filled corner we collected another brace of small chalk-stream fish.

Each apparently unfishable twist and bend required a different technique, each overgrown hatch-pool and shallow was approached using an established pattern with the rod held at just the right angle to drop a fly into the only available area of water. It was obvious that while the appearance of the stream had altered during the tenancy of my fishy friend, the quality of the fishing had not gone back.

To the utter dismay of our obstacle-course fisherman, we have started to make the water look presentable. We are trimming the trees on one bank straight down into the water, lopping off all the overhanging branches. The brambles in the hatch-pools have been pulled out and burnt.

The accumulated debris and ingrowing banks have been pulled out to dry and be burnt later. The cutting of the weed and the general stream clearance is dropping the water levels and turning the swampy sides into firm walking.

Everything begins to look as if someone has been about, but where have the fish gone? The trout from under the alders have retreated under what weed we have left. The hatch-pool can now be looked into like a goldfish bowl, causing the trout to mill around and seek new hiding-places.

I am beginning to hope that whoever buys this stream will let it revert to the fishing it was.

Battle of the Bugs

Weed is now being cut – flat-bottomed boats with paddles spinning on their sterns shuffle their way downstream, clearing the bed, disturbing those runs between the weed, spreading what little water there is out over the full extent of the river and slowing the pace of the stream almost to a standstill.

Weed left to grow and die in its own time fulfils a purpose in the food cycle of the year. A lot of river life knows no other home. It relies on weed movement in the currents to live a mobile life while being immobile itself, clinging to the weed.

In these late weed-cuts, when giant diggers work ceaselessly from weed boom to large factory-size heap on the bank, the boom-digger bucket and weed pile crawl with disturbed life. Most of this dies on the bank, but some drifts on to a fresh home on weed below the boom, only to have that cut from under them as the weed-boat chops its way downstream.

There was a lot of sense in the old river-keepers when they used to work their way upstream disturbing the river life but once. Massive weed-cuts in this river are done in the name of land drainage and in this chalk country to clear a way for the remote chance of a summer flood.

Sometimes I think it is just to find work for the Water Authority's machinery.

Low water and high river temperatures bring trouble to the hatchery. In the confined space of small concrete ponds, salmon and trout fry cannot move to faster, better aerated and therefore healthier water, so when the bug of furuncolosis looks for its victims, these close-packed immature fish are the first to be found.

Each morning hundreds of dead are counted. Small apparently perfect fish, yet hidden inside them the ravages of this killer that comes with low warm water. Take one of these small fish to pieces and the intestine is found to be heavily inflamed, showing a blood-red colour.

If the little fish have sufficient resistance to survive this stage, the bug then bites deep into the muscular structures. These processes penetrate to the surface and produce swellings or boils that break out into the water with numerous bacteria, spreading the disease on to their neighbours in the pond.

Pity the hatchery worker who, with great affection for his charges, daily mixes his doses of salt to try and combat this disease. Yet as the trickle of water through the stew dilutes the dosage, so more bugs enter from the main river. It is an unending battle with Nature.

These same water conditions which create larger than normal areas of semi-stagnant water cause fish such as roach and pike — who like occasionally to linger — to suffer attacks from tail and fin rot. This is a disease caused by bacteria that like these conditions and it marks a low-water year on a large number of fish as if they had been branded by having their tails cut short to mark the event.

In the hatchery ponds bacteria eat away at the gill covers of the fry leaving them with no cover to their respiratory folds, deforming them so that in three or four years' time, when they take the angler's artificial and are brought to the landing-net, the experienced rod will say that this is a fish born in a low-water year.

I recently attended a meeting of our river association which yearly elects a member to the Water Authority. There he voices our moans on pollution, water abstraction and a hundred other problems that we feel should be put forward to the Authority.

At this meeting, representing dozens of clubs, thousands of anglers and hundreds of riparian owners, sixteen people sat down.

The chairman and committee were re-elected with a proposing, seconding and a general nodding among themselves. I wonder if this closed circuit, caused by an apathy in our Association, is general in bodies, or are we unique?

A Question of Levels

I'd have taken a bet it would rain on August Bank Holiday. Can you imagine the look on villagers' faces when those first heavy showers of rain landed in the dust of the gravel lanes of Wiltshire?

Miniature eruptions of chalk from the side of the road, the cause of distress to animals and humans, sore throats and dusty eyes, and now suddenly this rain that turned it into a porridge that clung to Land-Rover wheels in off-white sticky lumps.

The eels were not deceived. There was no lifting of the river levels, no small stream came into the main with even a hint of colour and the forest of reed struck above the river surface remained as upright as ever with only the occasional raft of duckweed slipping, turning away with the wind.

The eel trap has taken four or five eels per night, then while it was raining and dark, with no moon due for another four or five days, we stood in anticipation through until midnight. We rescued two wrigglers off the rack at about eleven o'clock, another one just after midnight, then gave up all hope of a continued run.

Eels are large this year. The run that didn't take place last year is having its effect in the stay-over of the eel population into this year. What will happen if the right night doesn't come soon, or maybe for several years? Will they survive in the river once that trigger of migration instinct is touched off, or will they feed on and eventually send an army of monsters downstream? The average size of eels migrating in the Avon was 1½ lb, touching 2 lb this year. What of next year?

I stood on Charlton Shallows with an evening angler, waited until the last glimmers of dusk had settled, waited for the evening rise of Blue Winged Olive to set salmon parr, grayling and trout feeding – and waited in vain.

Bar one or two very splashy small dace there weren't enough BWO to attract. Maybe there weren't any fish.

BWO live in the gravel, spend their life feeding on the shallows, and are one of the casualities of this drought year. The area of their life has been reduced, their efforts concentrated and the fish that feed on them concentrated still further.

Sedges, caddis that crawl along the river's edge, seem to have vanished. One can remember other Septembers with a hovering carpet of brown that shifted in every direction at once. That was the sedge male waiting for the female to lift off the water. Then, when evening came, they would land on the reeds and slip into the water as they died.

One used to be able to search out large trout that worked their way along the margins of the water, seeing the pinprick of a rise of these delicate feeding fish that looked on sedge as their evening meal. They were always robust and well-fed and, after that moment when the surprise of the hook had rendered them still, they would tear across the water, and as it was usually getting dark, there was always the excitement of putting the landing-net in the right place.

But the sedge has gone, together with the small Cinnamon and the larger Welshman's Button, the caperer that used to drag itself across the water followed by a bow-wave of a chasing trout. Yet when wind caught the artificial in similar fashion and dragged the fly there was no response, no deceiving of fish.

I was persuaded to try the Test, to fish for grayling in the middle waters, where weed is cut and what flow there is remains distributed across the width of the river. Where the mention of duckweed on that aristocratic water makes them look askance.

But there was no flow, so I toss away the leaded nymph and fish downstream with a Palmer-tied fly. That, fishing wet, sinks like a stone. It catches on the underlying weed and can truly be called 'wet'.

Turn round and fish upstream, marshal a few grayling before you like a sheepdog until twenty or thirty are at double rod's length ahead, then you can pick them out by size with a carefully cast Lunn's Particular.

They have no more water than we, these people from the River Test. It's just that they have gardened their river into the realms of respectability. They have cut their weed and trimmed their banks so that flow is not hidden.

I saw a dozen grass-snakes at different places. I saw them submerge and retreat under the water, as if the dry uplands did not favour them and they needed the damp of the river basin. There are more rats about. It's as if everything has come down off the height of chalk downs and made the river a meeting-place.

You walk through some rough herbage and fallow deer are running before you see them stand. And forest ponies have broken out of the desert of the New Forest and stand pathetically on the river bank seeking food not obtainable in their forest.

In all this upset with the weather, things are being reversed that are going to take years to put right. Those small streams that run off the chalk below Shaftesbury into the Blackmore Vale have remained constant. There is no explaining it: a million and a half gallons per day in one spring, bubbling out with not one small variation in its flow — the stream line below a gash of green into the clay.

There is a lesson here to those water engineers on the River Thames who say they can't explain the sudden leak in the river-bed that is depriving the Thames flow of so many million gallons. What is more natural than that where these springs come off high ground they bubble through the bed of the river, which is why the river was formed that way.

Why shouldn't they reverse as the water table falls and takes water back into the land? There is a spring below the Road Bridge at Longford that in the height of water-tables cleans a vortex of river-bed, and yet when the river levels fall you can see the weed bending into it as the flow goes the other way.

The Magnificent Barbel

We have been without rain for so long that only the chalk hills above us, holding a reservoir of water, keep the river alive. Weirs are blocked off with flash-boards and main hatches are down to what leaks round the sides. It is possible to walk across the bed of the stream in wellingtons where once the float was set at 4 ft over dace and grayling.

One month I see my house surrounded by water and ducks feeding in the garden, the next month village wells run dry and the water-meadow cattle walk knee-deep in mud to drink.

Low water washes no soil from the banks or bed, sediment that is in suspension settles and the water clears so that the bed is revealed like a giant aquarium. Fish drift sideways as you approach, seeking to hide in any weed that remains. These clear water conditions tend to prove, or disprove, the reputation of some swims. We have long been suspicious that some hold larger fish than we imagine, and our imaginations are pretty fertile. We have a small enclosed pool in which there are some seven barbel, half a dozen good trout and a few dace. All these except the barbel have grown up there from fry. The barbel were gathered from various places and are fed on the residue of the hatchery. The best fish at one time weighed 11 lb, but I think he has gone back a little since then.

He comes to the surface like a trout, taking floating bread and entering into competition with other fish as to who can scoop up the most maggots when, in the evening, our anglers empty the remains of their bait-boxes to him. His large drogue-like mouth gaping in the clear water is a sight that is not easily forgotten.

He is the yardstick by which we judge all other barbel. We say they are bigger than the one in the stew — or almost — or much smaller.

Two of my anglers fishing a hatch-pool, where low water had closed the hatches and reduced the depth to about seven feet, enjoyed the clarity by dangling minnows in front of large perch. They were able to watch the shoal cruise round the pool and left their minnows in the shoal's path.

They were enjoying good sport when three large barbel entered the pool. All three dwarfed our captive in the stew, but one in particular will for ever make all others seem small. The three cruised the pool and in that clear water gave a display of how they feed. A sudden surge, a turn on the side and that wide open seaside-bucket mouth ploughed through the minnow shoals. All fishing elsewhere came to a stop and that little pool became surrounded by marvelling anglers.

Minnows, small dace and grayling were legered in the path of these cruising fish. As we watched I marvelled at the sense shown by these barbel. Lines leading down to baited hooks were avoided and circled as if they were obstructions. Various baits lying on the gravel caused the fish to detour a yard on either side. If this is the way large barbel live, then no wonder the record weight stays so small.

Towards evening it was noticed that some of the bread lying on the bottom was being picked up, so all baits were changed to egg-sized pieces of flake. One of the anglers watched the biggest fish of all go slowly up to his bait, take it and move off. He struck and had the fish on. Twenty minutes later the tiring fish was gently eased towards the largest salmon net available.

Flat on the surface its depth and size were plain to see; no estimate of its weight was put below 20 lb. Then the hooks pulled out and the fish swam slowly off to join its two friends to continue the circling of the pool. Within a short time we watched the fish start to feed again so a renewed effort was made to catch this magnificent barbel.

One of the anglers was actually disppointed when he saw one of the smaller fish pick up his bait, yet when this fish was landed it weighed-in at 12 lb 4 oz. On any other day, at any other time, it would have given cause for celebration, yet it raised no stir among us. It was so small compared with the one that had won its fight for freedom a short time before.

I have now opened the hatch into that pool, sending about 40 million gallons a day through it. Not much water by our standards, but enough to break up the surface and give this splendid fish some sort of protection.

Part 3: Autumn

Caught With His Pants Down

If ever I decide to start a River-keepers' Union, recruiting will be no problem. This cottage of mine seems to have developed into their meeting-place and a sorting-house for all the south-country river gossip.

This morning when I was settling down to answer letters two of my fellow keepers hindered progress for an hour or more. They sat and talked of their year's programme, of the way their employers viewed the passing year and their hopes for the coming one. One of them talked of the declining salmon in his river and of having to look elsewhere for fishing revenue. He planned to set up a trout hatchery and to convert his fishermen to the dry fly.

This particular keeper's water has a large head of coarse fish – grayling, roach and chub abound in every hole and run – yet at no time has his employer considered raising money from the sale of this type of fishing. But with the problems involved in stocking trout into this sort of company, I fancy he will get round to it sooner or later.

The keeper told me a story about one of his rods that I think bears repeating. About four hundred yards below a busy main road an elderly fisherman hooked a large salmon. This he played for about ten minutes, gradually tiring the fish out.

When it seemed he was near to grassing it and the fish was within a yard or two of the bank, it nosed its way gently into a large bed of weed, and there, with its tail protruding out of the weed patch, it resisted all attempts by the fisherman to pull it free.

So as not to lose such a good fish the salmon angler stripped down to his pants and vest and, with his gaff as a wading staff and rod held high, he attempted to dislodge the fish from its holt.

In this he was successful – in fact so successful that the fish took a new lease of life and ran upstream the four hundred yards to a pool immediately below the busy town bridge.

There, with a gallery of passing motorists and casual strollers, he landed his fish one-handed – the other hand was holding his underwear in place!

A weir pool on my water is a most popular fishing spot. It holds a good head of dace and grayling and quite a few chub are taken from the back eddy at the side of the pool. For reasons I have never been able to understand, it doesn't hold salmon.

Around the 1700s engineers replanned and landscaped the valley with a series of weirs. From my local market town almost to the sea they drove oak piles deep into the bed of the stream, heightening the water levels to give a mill a head of water or to push the river into the meadows. Cartloads of stone and gravel were dumped in front to form these ancient weirs. They were paved with stones tied together with iron clamps, which in turn were covered with molten lead, sealing the joint almost as completely as any modern device.

On my weir some of these stone blocks have in recent times shown increasing gaps along their edges. Seeking a reason for this movement of the weir crest I spent an hour or so with my aqualung, investigating, mapping and poking about deep under the weir.

The original oak piles had rotted off between the bed of the river and where they disappeared into the body of the weir, causing a deep scour some 4 ft into the base. In this dark cavity, out of sight and in perpetual shadow, were a number of large chub, far larger than have been caught from the pool in recent years.

Remembering that everything seen in the water through a face mask is one third larger than life, nevertheless some of those chub that hovered in the semi-dark were fish that had rarely taken a baited hook.

A shoal of wonderful perch, uniform in size, escorted me everywhere I went. And as I squeezed myself among a jungle of old piles they came along like sharks' pilot fish. Their colouring when out of water never shows up as well as when viewed from this angle.

Our Water Authority engineers, for ever co-operative, viewed the impending disaster as if it were an everyday occurence. My amateurishly drawn maps of the weir's underpinning were nodded at and I was told that this was no more than they had expected.

This weir had been the third – all built around the eighteenth century – to either turn over or to show that it was about to, and that if timbers of other weirs had gone, then it was about time this one followed suit!

Marauders

Now's the time when young seagulls come up-river and suddenly see ponds of helpless fish, so through July and August into September we bang away at the young birds.

We use carbide fed as gas into a chamber and sparked to explode at intervals. This, reinforced with a 12-bore and the finest size of shot, gradually teaches the birds to avoid the farm. They fly upstream and swing out into a wide avoiding arc so that in the shortest possible time they have been taught the rights and wrongs of life. It certainly works with seagulls whose single alarm cry passes on information to brothers and friends and means more than half a morning's lectures on how to survive.

However, it doesn't seem to mean the same thing, or happen the same way, to the mink. They scurry round the encroaching watercress beds and skirt the clear water in the boundary between weed-bank and river. With nose in the air and inquisitive eyes watching, the mink plumps in among the captive fish and feeds.

The very act of dropping into the crowded ponds sends the fish into a panic wave of trout pushing water before them so that it slops up the side of the stew and retreats through the grass leaving dozens of fish marooned. It then rolls back to the other end, gains momentum as water in a bucket will, and another dozen fish die in the roadway.

Oblivious to the distress, the mink sits and eats and chatters at the keeper as he thumbs the safety-catch off the 12-bore. There is no way that a lesson in survival can be learned by the dead corpse of this multi-coloured predator.

During these last weeks the litters have been breaking up and venturing outside parental control. They have sat on the feed-bags in the store-shed and viewed the young fish-farm workers with so little consideration that they would sleep if not prodded.

During this same period young herons barely lift their heads as you walk towards them. They step out of the way of the Land-Rover and learn in the bitter light of experience.

It's not only the feathered or four-legged creatures that need teaching. When the summer holidays hit local schools, there is a fresh crop of youngsters each year to fill in time through long summer days. Mothers with no time to spend on them turf them out with little idea of what they are going to do that day.

A small tubby child, with short legs that twinkled as he ran, vanished as I caught a glimpse of him through the trees. He sank into the ground like some wayward Indian and was only flushed out of dwarf privet by the inquisitive nose of an alsatian. He moved through the bushes with long-practised expertise and took the six-foot wooden fence like an Olympic hurdler leaving the dogs sniffing at his heels. He left behind him all the small treasures painfully gathered from his pocket money. A small six-foot solid fibre-glass rod and a junior fixed spool reel.

No doubt he'll come and collect them in due course, will accept the telling-off as payment for getting his tackle back, and will learn, as the herons and gulls learn, that the broadside aimed in his direction is to make him avoid certain places, to be more cautious in his way of life.

I bought one of those machines that makes a noise when it passes over metal. When we dig some holes in the ground in which to store fish there are long-lost pipes and such-like that we need to avoid, hence this strange-sounding instrument that buzzes when it detects.

I was not content to use it just for the technical work, for according to its brochure there was treasure under every tree. It reminded me that a million coins a year go missing and have done since the year dot and that the riverbank was a highway before the days of roads.

In the drought of 1976, markings among the crops showed Iron Age settlements very close to the river, while just down the road there were ornamental gardens from a long-lost manor house with gravel paths and such-like showing in the crop markings. But I know now that the main hobby of the last two or three hundred years was burying nails in the river-bank and that to every dozen nails somebody had added a rod-rest and rusting hooks, the ferrules from long-lost rods, metal keepnet rings — the list could go on unendingly. I've got a bucketful of unidentified material that contains more bottle-tops than anything else and one wonders where the empty bottle that once partnered the stopper has gone.

When the grasses and corn are flattened and the stubble is burnt and those long-forgotten paths that lead down to the river become exposed again, who knows what we may find?

Last week we thought we had found a sword from the wars of a thousand years ago. It turned out to be an old knife used in the cutting of weed from the buttresses round the hatches that we had lost ourselves within the last ten years. Somehow it had managed to get itself buried under six inches of earth.

A Lost Weekend

I am often told by fishermen that they have seen an eel of tremendous proportions under a bridge, or have hooked and lost one. Weights of eight to ten pounds are mentioned without a thought in their minds about exaggeration or story-telling. Yet the eels which come down into the trap, which every migrating eel must eventually come to, do not reflect anything like the sizes of eels lost to anglers.

I sometimes think those see-through-the-water spectacles made to personal prescription magnify as well as take away the water glare. People come and say they have seen a 40 lb salmon under a certain tree. I go and look and venture the opinion that it is only 20 lb or even less. They then poke a pair of these spectacles at me and suggest I do a reappraisal – and sure enough the fish grows.

It was an angler who normally talks sense who started this sort of thing off again with some big trout he had seen. They weighed up to 10 lb, he said – three of them at the mouth of the pipe where the hatchery waste enters the river. Being busy with other things I let the story sit in my mind with the big salmon and the 20 lb barbel, putting a question mark and a 'perhaps' against them.

Then another angler, a bit of a character, in babbling Welsh accent, doubled the size of the trout from the estimates of the previous angler and swore they were salmon, feeding on the minnows in and at the mouth of the pipe.

It was with some scepticism that I was persuaded to go and look – and they were right to within a pound or so if the fish were as deep as we believed. Two feet long, with tails like the double spread of your hands, the fish moved in and out of the pipe with mouths open, chomping away on packed minnow

shoals as they browsed into the thick of them. Three brown trout that needed no prescription spectacles to assist the excitement of their bulk.

I dropped all thoughts of work and became, for two lost days, a specimen hunter. I did the obvious thing and added one minnow to the shoals, a minnow on a hook attached to 8 lb line. Those trout went past the line as if negotiating a roundabout, avoiding the slightest contact with what looked like a wire hawser in the foot of clear water.

I scaled down to 4 lb line in a ridiculous attempt at deceit, with no more success, though with the added realization that these fish were as near human as intelligence could make them. Why else should they ignore us standing as near as three yards away with the rod tip wagging above them like a London dock crane?

We legered a minnow, tried to get them feeding on bread, watched them into the evening and saw the largest one of all pause in his minnow meal and take an hors d'oeuvre of Blue Winged Olive. So out came the fly rod and a delicate winged creation was landed gently on his nose. But by then he was back on his main meal of minnow and the morsel of fly life didn't recompense him for the energy used. I say him, for all three were cock fish with kipes like gaffs.

Can you imagine the biggest, liveliest lobworm drifting wriggling past a trout's nose and the fish not turning towards it even by the slightest hint, not even acknowledging that he had seen it go wriggling past the corner of his mouth? Even when they landed on his nose and for a moment draped themselves across his vision they were totally ignored.

A small boy of our acquaintance waded cold-footed in the small chalk stream and came back with a dozen reasonably sized crayfish. They were allowed to crawl freely, with the smallest of trebles tied gently to their undersides.

They dug themselves under stones and followed the minnows up the pipe, they crawled across the cleaner gravel and in that shallow water used the bulk of one of the huge fish as shade from the light. They were completely ignored.

We thought of going into the outfall run-out and lowering a bait into the pipe itself, but that would have been a useless effort. I waded into the dark and floated every sort of fly in the box over their general vicinity, being kept on my toes by the tiniest of dimple rises that could have been them or one of the minnows they sat among.

Talk about a lost weekend, or fish-fever! I had two days of it and two nights of nightmares in which those trout grew to such a size that their kipes projected, into my dreams.

On my finishing-room wall sits the Avon's record trout of 16½ lb, mouth slightly open, artificial eye peering down, thinking his status is secure. But I've promised him that his position is temporary.

Memories of Youth

They say, don't they, that you must never go back. More years ago than I care to remember I roamed the Cumberland fells with rod, gun and dog, more wild than the sheep that scattered from the path.

I knew every pool and cascading gulley in the three rivers that ran into the sea at Ravenglass. I followed the sea-trout shoals as they edged in from the salt and took a toll each evening from the shifting fish. The local with his click hook — a poacher's device not unlike a flying gaff — belly down on the grass, was a constant companion in each well-stocked pool.

If this has a sound of the Lakelands and a nagging urge within me to go back, then forgive me, for it is my youth that I am getting mixed up with and young days always seem better days.

Last week I went back. The telephone people gave me the number of the small village pub where a peal (sea-trout) slid across the counter was always good for a half-pint.

As I remember it then, fifteen shillings a week plus two bob walking allowance didn't allow me to become involved in the local night life too much. I phoned. Yes, they had a room and would I confirm. I did. The excitement I felt was as if it was my first fishing trip again.

It's hard to say when the first disillusioning started — perhaps it was the heavy traffic and long queues at the end of the M6. Or maybe the single-track roads widened to take the sightseeing coach.

Perhaps it was the hotel itself which had lost its small beer-stained bar for a posh restaurant sign in burnt oak, or maybe the bedroom down the street, across the road a hundred yards away. The receptionist, not there in my day, said, 'The annexe, sir.'

Things weren't quite as I remembered. Still, the food was good and I did see trout jumping in the bay from my bedroom window. There was still the same smell of mud and salt down the village street.

A new keeper there now. He netted the salmon garth each tide and did little better than old Peg-Leg who did the same job in my time. He didn't fish, this new keeper, so had not the store of knowledge that an angler would have had, but he kindly permitted me to look around.

But things had changed. On a river where another angler had been a rare sight, each pool was now surrounded with umbrellas, rested rod and legered worm, lines crossing in the middle. Each side fished out towards the far bank and the shy sea-trout were huddled down the centre under an arch of crossed nylon. With the bright sun and gin-clear water, surely the only chance of catching any would come in the night.

Another river, the Esk, had still the same appearance of a well-stocked stream. Two salmon and a shoal of peal quartered a pool in uneasy restlessness, but there the resemblance died.

Once the banks were wild and the not-so-clever angler could hide out of sight and mind of fish. Now those same banks had the appearance of a railway terminal, bare and desolate, where any movement against the sky was registered immediately by a shock wave through the assembled fish.

Bridge-leaning, I watched three modern tourists, motorcycles leaning against the buttress. They worked away at bringing boulders off the bank in an attempt to alter the look of the river. With great enthusiasm they shifted tons of rock to create a new pool and then with the intervention of a Cumberland Water Authority bailiff, they were made to move it all back again.

In my day, I would have been glad of the company of three such workers.

I asked a farmer if he still possessed a pickle barrel and he didn't even know what I meant. (Salmon hooked off the redds in the middle of winter were hung whole in a barrel of brine and fed to dog and hired hand when food was short.)

To some extent faith in memories was restored when I

wandered the smallest river of the three. Its narrow width and shallow pools could have held little interest for the visitor with fish in mind, for here the banks were rough and the angling was as I remembered it.

It rained in the night and those lobs that I collected down in Wiltshire were used along the edge of a typical Lakeland spate. The fish were there in numbers as well as something that took a worm and headed back through the estuary towards the Isle of Man, taking fifty yards of line with it.

Leaving well alone, I packed, paid my bill and went and fished water that wasn't part of my youth.

The Livebait Smugglers

We are reminded of the rustlers of old, of lights in the night and goods smuggled across boundaries. Legislation that has lain idle for a couple of years is being brought into the open.

Water Authority rules make it illegal for anyone to move fish or ova without permission. We are not to take the spawn of trout or any other freshwater fish more than the length of a cricket pitch without a certificate of health and reliability. And this does not just apply to fish farms, this means *you*.

You will commit an offence if you take a bucket of livebait down the road and fish in another water, and should you pick up a dozen crayfish on the upper Avon and use them on the lower, you will have committed an offence.

The movement of livebait has been responsible for carp in the River Itchen, chub in the Test and bream in the Avon. Weekly somebody comes down from London without being sure of his ability to catch dace for livebait and brings half a dozen fish in a plastic container from some source near the metropolis. And I would hate to think of how many of our fish go in the reverse direction to the upper Thames and the various gravel-pits spread around the home counties.

New carp lakes constructed in the Wessex area were quietly stocked by means of a bit of thieving, anglers from the club involved being persuaded to bring home their catch, even poaching to meet the necessary stocking level.

I met a gentleman on the Shaftesbury lakes with a plastic

bucket full of fry, 67 three-inch mirror carp, heading out illegally from the water. I accused him of stealing and had all the indignity of long words and a thorough education slapped back in my face.

How difficult it is to say that those fish are mine when the poacher is articulate and claims them as God's bounty. I explained that the ponds he had taken them from were as artificial as the goldfish pond in the back garden of his own house. That the carp in them were bought and paid for by the same reasoning as his own goldfish were paid for in jam-jars.

It was like battering your head against a brick wall to talk of the privacy of property while standing on the edge of a wide open field, with hedges and barbed wire, and try to liken it to paved road and garden fences.

I frightened him with this new awareness of mine concerning the restrictions of moving fish and told him that if we prosecuted in court, the Water Authority would show an interest in his action. The loss of a few fry wouldn't have worried me so much but this week when we drained down to do some sort of autumn stocktaking, we found that somebody had pinched a 27 lb mirror carp from one of the ponds. They had either taken her home for a good Eastern European baking or she resides as another bit of illegal movement in a new lake. If things go on as they are we shall have to brand every fish or paint them a specific colour so that we may know our own.

Carp fry seem to be plentiful and one or two farms that are moving into the production of these fish have had a good year.

Artificial stripping is being developed in this country, following the European pattern, while the Dubisch pond with its warm water pan is being varied with deeper lakes and shallow margins where the water can be drained away from the spawning area, then the hatched egg protected by weld-mesh fencing.

We drained a nursery pond through a catching area and ran thousands of fry into holding tanks and I showed my ignorance in believing that the tench had crossed with the mirror carp.

I thought that these greeny smooth-scaled fry were a by-product of a mixed population pond but apparently they are the leather carp which has the same parentage as the mirror, developing its scales in a different fashion.

The greed of the heron and the damage he can do was demonstrated when the lakes were drained and it was necessary to leave them overnight with the dorsal fins of hundreds of fish showing above the surface. Next morning five carp between 1½ lb and 3 lb were lying on the mud. Two were still alive and all were stabbed through the body — fish far beyond the heron's ability to swallow.

One for the Book

Still it rains. What was once a drought year is now an autumn spate. At no time over the last month or so has the river had time to recover its composure. It rains, I lift a hatch and let the extra water downstream, then that opened hatch becomes permanent as more rain arrives to lift the levels still further.

Debris from a long summer washes down from the upper reaches. Discarded oil drums from some non-country-loving person hang against the weed-racks till pulled out, or kicked on through to the next beat downstream.

My cottage stands within the flood plain, half an inch above the high-water mark left by the 1961 floods. As the weather is at the moment the river could be at the bottom of my kitchen table instead of at the bottom of the garden.

This morning was the start of the last day of this year's salmon season. Our total catch for the year stood at an odd number, needing but one fish to round the figure and make our record book seem a little better.

So this morning for an hour I fished. In front of the hatches I threw a No. 3 spinner in all directions with no response from the fish that I knew lay there. I trundled my bait under the willows into the eddies and under the roots. My enthusiasm was that of the end of the year, not of the spring.

Half-way through the morning I was joined by one of my syndicate members, a G.P. long retired. Our interest in the fish needed to round off the season waned as we thumbed through this bad season's memories.

We talked of the fish we had lost when all seemed right, of sudden takes, screaming reels and rod tips pulled down deep into the water. As is right when this mood of reminiscing is on us, we sat and watched the river. The cattle on the bank seemed as interested as we were in something midstream. Perhaps they had been fishermen in some previous life.

A dorsal fin, followed by a large gently waving tail parted the water in front of us. Here was the fish we needed. We moved back and round so as to get well in front of him, taking our time to allow this fish to return to his lie and be settled down before we showed him the bait.

But this was not to be. He was restless. He heaved himself three feet out of the water, landing on his side, sending waves rolling into the river margins, dancing the floating cress and showing himself to be as stale a fish as is possible for this time of the year. He rose from the stream-bed and took a small sparsely dressed fly with the daintiness one associates with dace. His fight was short and mostly on the surface, full of splash and short half-determined runs for cover.

We could not gaff him as this is not allowed on my river after the end of August, so he was tailed on to the bank where the staleness of him really showed. His deep red flank, covered with a multitude of spots, was scarred from the knocks he had received as he had driven himself through the river's numerous weirs.

The hook was where it should be, in his scissors, its hold on the fish light and easy to break. We needed a fish this day, tomorrow was too late, but not so badly as to kill this river veteran on the threshold of spawning.

We held him upright in the current, his mouth and gills working to recover the oxygen used in a useless fight. Then he slid away upstream, showed once twenty yards on, then nothing. I may see him again later this year when he will be one of a gang behind, or accompanying, some hen fish in the fast water on the redds.

So the salmon season is over for this year and one more fish would have made my total look more respectable. Still, the trout year has been good and the roach, chub and the rest of the coarse fish will not let us down in the rest of the year.

A Day With 'The Boys'

You cannot know the feeling, but I was fed up with fish. Everywhere I went — fish. Everything I did — fish. Every conversation I had — fish. So taking up a friend's invitation, I drove the 200 miles to Fishguard and took a ferry across to Ireland. What for? To see more fish, of course!

I got off to a bad start by being seasick during the three-hour crossing, then the hire car taking me inland had a series of punctures. Those quiet roads are something wonderful when you are used to our crowded race-tracks, but it is difficult to appreciate them when you are trundling along on a flat tyre and the last garage was six miles back.

I was offered a lift by one of those little carts pulled by a donkey that was smaller than my alsatian dog, but as I was passing him even with a flat tyre there seemed little point.

When I did get to the fish farm I expected to see an overgrown site of long grass, bushes and clogged screens due to economies of labour — but not a bit of it.

Two hundred sheep keep the grass looking like the MCC cricket ground and there's a little income from the mutton. I saw sheep on their knees eating grass where it grew out of water. For the fish there was no feeding three, four or five times a day. The farm used self-feeders — half the price and three times as good as any others I have seen. These, filled once a day, kept fish happy and did away with tables of so many pounds according to temperature and fish densities.

I spend a lot of time keeping people away from my ponds, but here they are welcomed, paying at the gate for admission and a small plastic bag of fish food that goes a long way towards keeping those ponds near the gate well-fed.

One stew that attracted most of the visitors was a pond full of rainbow trout of great size — ten to twelve-pounders massed together in unbelievable density. I was tempted to slip a couple into my suitcase!

They have some trouble with the grey crow and the occasional otter, but so great is the number of fish that this is a small wastage. After a couple of days of learning and drinking the wine of the country — a dark, black liquid — I was asked if I would like to have a day with 'The Boys'.

The invitation came out of the dark corner of the bar from an Irish voice that could have belonged to any of the half-dozen faces turned in my direction. I didn't know them, they didn't know me, but we had told each other stories from both sides of the fishing trade for some hours and while we didn't use quite the same methods, the end product was the same.

Three of them agreed to meet me the next morning in a small bar attached to the farm. The system of attaching a bar to small shops and businesses — e.g., undertaker-and-bar, newsagent-and-bar — is such a civilized custom that we should take it up. Who knows, river-keeper-and-bar!

We met perhaps too early; it needed hours to get the sun in the right place, they said, so when we did go forth we were a happy gang.

With no apparent tackle we spent the rest of the morning peering into water from trees and high banks, well-worn tracks leading from one vantage point to the next. Salmon were there in plenty — red brutes of all sizes from six to thirty-odd pounds. But didn't they know a thing or two, those fish!

As the four of us moved from pool to pool, a shock-wave of panic went before us, a sort of 'here they come again' feeling passing among the fish. But don't get the idea that there was any inbred stealth exercised; it was more like a bunch of steers, tails upright, fleeing from the warble fly.

There was more excitement as bigger and better fish were spotted, then strange silences at some pools until an old friend they knew should be there was spotted.

I was worried about the water bailiffs and asked if we shouldn't be a little quieter and perhaps keep a little more out of sight? But those three Irish boyoes had forgotten me. They were doing something they had done many times before, something their fathers and grandfathers had done in this same prescribed way.

We came to an old farm bridge with more holes than planks and they ran to it at a rate that left me far behind and more than a little out of breath.

When I got there they were laid out like the remnants of a battle, the passage of cattle as recently as that morning ignored. A stick seven feet long was brought out of hiding from among the bridge girders and a gaff which had mysteriously appeared was being whipped to it.

I have seen salmon removed from most of our south country streams with great professionalism, not once but many times. I wish I could say the same for this occasion! They couldn't agree on the place to make the attempt, then they fought for the gaff and the privilege of using it.

At last, when all differences were sorted out, the fish had gone. Not willing to put up with the finesse of the previously mentioned bunch of steers the fish fled downstream like one of those Olympic canoes in the slalom.

The boyos charged after the fish, leaving the gaff hanging from the bridge, which was perhaps as well for at this point we were joined by another person who took a silent interest in our antics.

Suddenly we became ordinary God-fearing river-watchers with no more interest in fish than to see them swim. With visions of my short stay in the country being prolonged in prison, the illegal instrument was spirited away and a hurried relationship cemented at the salmon-pool bar.

Francis J. Ryan, our silent watcher, has been in salmon and trout protection for more than twenty years and very little wool is pulled over his eyes. As fishery inspector for the River Suir and the fresh water portion of the River Nore, he has seen it all. Nets, gaffs and Cymag have all been tried in his area more than once and some of the tales he tells me make me glad he didn't come along a little sooner.

I stayed on for another two days' trouting, finding conditions much the same as on our own small chalk streams. Clear water and stacks of small trout to take the dry fly. Everyone worms with salmon in mind; it's a bait the trout and coarse fish seem to have learned to avoid except when there is colour in the water. But they haven't quite got on terms with a well cocked-up olive put down a couple of inches in front of their noses!

Menace or Mouse?

Alsatian dogs have had some adverse publicity of late. Somebody gets bitten and from that moment on every alsatian that raises a growl gets his picture and story in the press. The dogs are trained to bite and surprise is shown when they do just that.

We had a couple of poachers the other day, fishing the holy of holies near the trout farm. So gathering a couple of these fierce dogs we made them sit a hundred yards away while we took the names and addresses of the two intruders, the sitting dogs menacing, as it were, from a distance and needing but a whistle to bring them into confrontation — or so it would have seemed.

With one eye on the sitting dogs, the two poachers walked past, going back to their vehicle. As they did so one burst into laughter that progressed from hysteria to complete collapse. His companion, puzzled for a while, joined him in what looked like a hidden pocket of laughing gas.

Then we found the cause of their hilarity. In our hurry to get down to the river we had collected one alsatian dog from the house, opened the back door of the van and gestured him inside without paying much attention to what he might have in his mouth.

Now he sat in the field taking an interest in what was going on — with a rubber mouse in his mouth, a plaything from his puppy days that squeaked when he closed his mouth, a reassuring noise that assisted him in passing the time between gallops 'twixt kitchen and garden!

A guard dog with a squeaky mouse loses all appearance of menace, especially when he tries to persuade a poacher to throw it so that he can retrieve it!

Wandering in Wales

Suddenly it's the end of summer. The bright dreams of spring are long gone, there is a yellow tinge to the leaves on the oak and the light underside of the aspen poplar is something less than white.

I saw a child dancing through the village, collecting twelve leaves for twelve happy months next year and, like the London to Brighton Old Crocks' Run, it seemed only last month that I last saw it happen. There is a shift in the air, a move towards winter with just a pause for autumn.

I sat on a hillside in Wales. A few scrubby trees, dying bracken, the sound of falling water and, in the distance, fox-hound music. Some unfortunate litter of cubs was being taught the realities of a foxy life. The small stream in the bottom of the valley, blown up by overnight rain, had its normal sheep road along its way — a thin hard path that picked the easy line downhill past small pools, steep water and sea-trout with the push of autumn spawning in their tail. They going one way, I the other.

There were fallow buck on the hillsides and the crack of a rifle, then up the hillside came one of those mustard — coloured, four-wheel-drive, go-anywhere-without-legs Range Rovers. I was the biter bit, the keeper trespassing. I was a good hundred yards from a footpath and the irate gentleman, accompanied by keeper and rifle with telescopic sight, looked like something from a last-war film. Was I fishing, poaching, or allowing Spinner, the alsatian, to chase sheep?

'I am a keeper,' I told them, and over the top of their slight interest showed some of my own at the four-pointed antlered deer, mouth agape and tongue lolling out, in the back of the vehicle.

Back on the footpath but now well away from the water, I 'hallooed' a travelling fox and joined Spinner in a brief hunt over the top and a cold seat on the shady side of the hill. Hounds streamed past in pursuit of a bedraggled quarry.

Out of the hotel next morning I turned south instead of east and followed the same stream towards the mining areas of South Wales — the same name to the valley but now twice the width and not quite the pace to the stream.

Its colour had gone and there was more depth. There were no sea-trout showing at the falls, but humped fishermen crouched between the boulders, sitting quietly. As still as a heron under the alders I avoided all stupid thoughts of asking 'What luck?'

There is no finer culler of game than the Welshman. When my father gamekeepered in that heathen country they put gin-traps between the potato rows to take the pheasant, and their use of the worm when the sea-trout is inexperienced is a poem of perfect fishing.

To sit on a Welsh hillside, tired from a five or six-mile walk, and knowing you have the return journey to do, is to iron out all the wrinkles from a fish-saturated mind. I watched those short, stiff rods and worm tackles for half a day. I saw fish to 4 lb fight more in the air than in their natural element and watched the anglers put their harvest from the sea into plastic bags, then melt into the background of gorse and hillside.

I watched a hobby, a hawk slightly smaller than a kestrel but built more on the lines of a Harrier jet, able to pause a few inches above the ground and take a beetle, or dart through a thistle-eating pack of goldfinches, taking a bird without pausing in its line.

The hobby sat on a post in the pathside fence, cocking an eye at me as it plucked a small bird and then, getting tired of the job, ate it, feathers and all.

As the wind moved out of the south there was a smell of burning colliery tips and the drone of traffic that seemed to grow and loom nearer than it should be. Then came the same Range Rover as yesterday, keeper and employer plus rifle and telescopic sight, and I was out of bounds again — the footpath was over there across the hill.

Shades of that unwitting trespasser at home! I will treat you more considerately next time we meet. I wasn't allowed back the way I came and walked the six-mile alternative offered while they sat and watched that I went that way. Then I thought of those wormers in dark corners who were thumbing a nose at my unfriendly friends.

As an invited guest I spent a few hours on one of those well-stocked lakes towards the centre of Wales, caught a 1½ lb rainbow with my first cast and a 3 lb fish with the second. As I didn't need either I spent an hour making certain they would live. I propped the larger one up with a couple of bricks and fanned water through his gills as some sort of thank-you for the fight he put up and to apologize for the operation of having to remove a hook from three parts down his length. That's the last time I will fish for stocked fish put in the day before, unless I'm starving.

Walking in Wales is to walk with the sound of water dying behind you while another torrent of sound grows in front. Curlew and crow, then suddenly fifty youthful riders from a mid-Wales Activity Centre appear.

On a recreational holiday for young people, they turn up on their first day with fishing tackle, a saddle, or walking shoes and haversack. Wandering among them as they made the first hesitant casts into the trout lakes, I was reminded of the gulf that exists between these country-loving youngsters and the louts who riot mindlessly after, or before, a football match.

I got mixed up with a hundred or so of these open-air youngsters and, instead of questioning them, was torn apart with their anxiety to talk fish, their group enthusiasm and questing eye. Would that I had time to spend with them.

Mink Pays a Call

Autumn – leaves drifting in the current and circling through the eddies, gradually getting waterlogged so that soon all moving water becomes stained with their colour. The sun, lower in the horizon, lacks the power to lighten the water, leaving it dark and mysterious-looking, as the river should be at this time of the year.

The young of the valley have not yet become fully aware of the danger associated with humans. Herons that were hatched in the late spring watch my approach and only take to unhurried flight when my dogs begin to take an interest in their presence. This lack of caution is all right as long as they stay in this vicinity, but as they grow older and venture on to the chalk-stream tributaries their first lesson could be their last.

Daily the fishermen report wandering mink, obviously born this year. They show their lack of fear by walking up to and round the anglers as if they were no more than an addition to the river-bank. Once again their first lesson could be a hard one.

Waterfowl that competed for the anglers' groundbait, and for a few short months shared a friendly swim, have already discovered that they have been deceived.

Survivors from earlier flocks of mallard, teal and widgeon now take off in agitated flight, with many a look behind them as they go. To them the rod hold-all has the same silhouette as the 12-bore.

Ribbon weed left uncut by the searching knives is now covered with larvae of the reed smut, nymph of olive and caenis, and forms the basic food for the hungry chub and roach. The chub hovers in mid-water, gradually working the long strand of ribbon down so that at times he resembles an airship moored some way in front, then, reaching the end, drifts back and starts again on the next strand – meat and veg all in one go.

My newly opened stream has become more and more established. It is now quite normal to drive my aluminium boat right

into the garden, almost up to my fishing-room door. It has even been recognized by the Water Authority's weed-cutting boats. They churn up the main stream and, seeing water coming in from the side, turn and cut the weed in the new channel.

The good they do at the mouth is stirring it up, deepening it down to its gravel and widening it to the firmness of the fields.

The new stream has one disadvantage – it brings the river animals that much closer to my cottage. Sitting writing, and lifting my head to watch the wake of an animal swimming, I realized that a mink had come into the garden. Now my bitch Mona has a rare dislike for the mink. She will hunt him until she trees him and once treed it is a quick end, so whistling her to my heel we charged out to chase the intruder.

As I approached he was making his presence known to the fish population. They were leaving the water, skipping sideways and shooting in all directions. It was all too plain that he was making things very unpleasant down below. The mink is not able to stay submerged very long. He does not seem able to poke a nostril out of the water and take a quick breath as the otter does. When being chased he seems to prefer the herbage along the bank, only using the water as a quick place to dodge into.

This mink was a little different. He left the water, chased by the dog and various anglers who had joined the hunt, round the house and through the first open door into my fishing-room, through the fishing-room into the lavatory and there, sitting on the pedestal, he was netted.

Eels by the Ton

If I had deliberately picked my holiday date so that I skipped all the hard work I couldn't have done it better. While I sunned myself on the black volcanic beaches of the Canary Isles the monsoon season opened in England.

That slice of pie across Wales and England, across South Devon and Wessex, was as barren as the moonscape of Tenerife when I left. Then it rained four inches of water that in the space of a few days changed the colour of the landscape to green and, because the ground was still warm, produced a flush of grass that rivalled the spring of the year.

There were mushrooms by the million, created in an ideal atmosphere of moisture and 51 degrees Fahrenheit. A continual stream of people went out in the mornings, catching the crop as it grew, walking the river-banks in the mist and picking those large, dinner-plate horse mushrooms from beneath the willows.

The rain lifted all the accumulated rubbish of the past twelve months and brought it down like an escalator. Raft after raft of watercress and washed-out, extended bank. Willow trees that had rooted where they fell were lifted down into hatchways and then piled up solid with all the rubbish that the Salisbury citizens pitch into the river. Maybe it was because of the hot summer that so many bottles, containing the thirst-quenching qualities that anglers and swimmers need, were taken down to the river. Then, after slaking their thirst, they pitched their empties into the reeds. When flooded with this autumn rain, down came the reed — and bottles in their thousands.

If we could have taken them out and dumped them on somebody's doorstep we would have done so, but instead we had to watch them fall through the hatches on to concrete sills and then be washed down into the lower pool in a mass of broken, jagged glass. If this sort of thing continues and the throwaway society goes on, then the child who swims in a summer river will be a thing of the past.

We had a tree that took a tractor several hours of pulling and pushing before the suction of the hatches released it. Intermingled with this night-work — for somehow none of this awkward removal happens during the day — and the downstream trek of rubbish, came the expected flow of eels.

At a conservative estimate the rivers Itchen, Test and Avon took 20 tons of eels in that single night. I didn't mind missing the hard work involved with hatch-cleaning and the sending on of rubbish, but to be away when the largest run of eels for many years came down was a sad blow.

The previous one-night record was an eel-a-minute through a twelve-hour run. As each eel weighed 1½ lb on average and sold for something like 50p per pound, you can see that the night's work was well worth the effort. That was on three linked traps in a matter of four miles, but on this occasion the neighbouring trap took 84 eels in one recorded quarter of an hour and put an end for all time to any boasting of trap records.

A single trap on the Test, staffed by many eager hands, counted its turnover in tons, while another one on the Itchen refused to disclose its total catch, but had two large vehicles to take the haul to market.

One eel of 7¼ lb in a trap at Salisbury seemed to have been the largest from the south. There were many five-pounders and hundreds of four-pounders and these went to the smokers.

The wonder of it is that the Dutch eel collectors, with some sort of foreknowledge, were on the doorsteps of the larger fish catchers before the last eel had wriggled in. They boosted the price so that suddenly our own jellied eel manufacturers were struggling to compete.

There was a single salmon below the trap on the morning after — the last day of the salmon season. This one fish with a silver coat of the sea was head-and-tailing in fast water while half a dozen anglers cast to attract its attention.

Somehow there was no excitement, more a sense of sympathy in its migration. Perhaps it was the embarrassment felt among the anglers that they should queue up to try and inflict injury on this unique fish.

In the aftermath of rain with the river still two hatches strong, there is just that hint of colour in the water that makes for good fishing. There is not the autumn coolness yet, there has been no frost to take the leaves off the early poplar. In fact, the brown of autumn that crept into the leaves in September has taken more a look of spring, an increased greenness in the leaves as if they were trying to make up for time lost.

There are busy shoals of roach feeding at the mouths of the carriers with some dozen or so two-pounders caught within the past week or so and plenty of 40 lb bags. At the tail of the swims, barbel have shoaled and the yearly rumour of a fish twice the size of the present record seen with a look of contempt on its fishy face.

Night Fright

I have always believed that autumn is the best time of the year. There is none of the harshness of spring, of unexpected cold days and late frosts in March, but trees multi-coloured with their last few leaves trying to survive.

Work on the river bank involves the lopping of dying limbs and pulling out waterlogged trees. Then, when all labour has gone home, there is the soft smell of wood-smoke and blue haze drifting up between leaves losing their hold and slipping slowly to the ground.

The river, depleted of water, barely moves its carpet of this leafy debris downstream and the trout dimple safely out-of-season. The time to enjoy is when you can find reason to sit, wait and watch through those last few minutes of light into the darkness.

It was a float attached to a yard of line, in turn attached to one of my big stock rainbows, that gave me the reason and determination to sit into the night.

The dog-fox howling across the fields to attract a mate, thinking of the cubs that should be born next March, raises the hair on the back of your head as he comes closer, moving downwind without any suspicion that there are humans about. Suddenly some message in the air got to him and when his shouts started again they were five fields away.

The more that the night is involved with your life, the more our ancestors of a couple of thousand years ago touch you. Tales of silent things that creep and a child's terror in a dark wood mix with a Celtic background and it is easy to frighten the bravest of the brave.

Night-work means eel-trapping and security, sleeping in a caravan on the trout stews, both involved with things that go bump in the night. The dead sheep in the eel-trap and the herd of steers that broke their containing fence caused the alsatian dog sleeping in the open door of the caravan to climb into bed with me, shaking with fright.

As the night moved on, the north sky grew lighter from the street lamps of a nearby town. Silhouettes of bat and hunting owl crossed, and criss-crossed, each one causing the safety-catch on the 12-bore to be pushed forward.

Then from my right came a rustling in the long grass and a low, dark shadow a couple of feet high crept along the pond's margins. The village lights had gone out and the single street lamp on the nearby crossroads left a pit of shadow when it too went out.

Off went the safety-catch again, with thoughts of foxes.

Then, as the form crept nearer, my mind shifted to improbable animals. With only a whisper through the grass it moved nearer and I was forced to stand up and declare myself or to put two barrels into it and hope for the best.

A small child, no more than ten years old, was on hands and knees, dragging all the tackle in the world behind him. He screamed for help and he told me later that he nearly died of fright — though it was nothing to the fright he gave me.

The knowledge that a double-barrelled 12-bore with the safety-catch off had been pointed at a child will haunt me all my remaining years. I blame some parent for allowing him to be out after midnight at that time of the year. The taste for trout or a boyish sense of adventure must have been the spur.

An Identity Problem

Trout are beginning to accumulate in the fast water of the redds. Small patches of disturbed, clean gravel are beginning to show as hen fish, not quite ready to spawn, run forward and test the looseness of the gravel.

A few weeks without rain now would lift these redds high and dry out of the water. On the other hand, heavy rain would make this site just as unsuitable.

A month ago trout ran through to the upper reaches of the winterbourne, and now, after three weeks without rain, we have had to take the electric machine out and rescue them from the pitiful remnants of the high water. Three hours of working downstream on the three-quarter-mile stretch that was in danger of running dry produced 143 trout between ½ lb and 4½ lb. They were brought back and released in the mouth of a chalk stream where they are in no danger of running out of water.

I am always at a loss as to whether these fish that run so readily up the winterbourne and other small streams in the autumn are true brown trout or migratory sea-trout. Their colour is that of the brownie, although their spots tend to be larger with very little red among them. The silver of the sea-trout in the estuary bears no relation to the colour of the fish in the upper reaches.

I know that where we took those 140-odd trout last week,

a new lift in levels will bring a fresh run to fill each pool and lie with further fish. There must be a reservoir of trout somewhere in the main stream, estuary, or sea to sustain these numbers.

Keepers who rear their own trout are forever on the look-out for big healthy fish to strip into their hatchery. Eight or nine-pound cock-fish full of milt are a prize that they will use with selected hens at spawning time. So when a keeper friend of mine saw these large winterbourne fish a few years ago he scrounged the best of them for his hatchery.

I told him of my suspicions that some could quite well be from the sea so he gave them a thorough sorting out before using their eggs. He took any sign such as brightness of coat, shortness in length for weight, or thickness of wrist to mean sea-trout. The rest, all beautiful brownies, he stripped into his hatchery troughs. The resulting eggs were that lovely orange colour that you get from healthy wild fish; the eggs from his stew-fish were pale and anaemic in comparison.

Keeping the fry separate, he fed them up for twelve months with a diet of minced liver and fish offal. In the spring, their age now fifteen months, they ranged in weight between 3 oz and 7 oz.

As the month of April moved on, the yearling trout took to lining up at the outfall of the stews, individual fish making determined efforts to get away downstream. Their coats lost the brown-trout appearance and took on that of the sea-trout smolts.

Now, more than suspicious of what he had in the stew, this friend of mine carefully clipped the dorsal fin of each and every one of about a hundred fish. He then phoned me, told me what he had done and asked me if I would run my eel-trap which was situated ten miles or so downstream of the release point.

The following morning I had fifty marked fish in my storage box and for a week, among the normal run of smolts, they came with their clipped fins showing up among the others.

After a while I had nearly all of those hundred fish in my stew-ponds. As they were of no further use to the upper water I kept them for twelve months, releasing them when they were short, fat one to two-pounders.

Infiltrators

The first frosts were late. Not until November did we go out to find ice on the cow drinks and a firmness on the softer, muddier parts of the river-bank.

These first frosts of the winter, so necessary to the gamekeepers, strip the last leaves off the trees and kill any further thought of growth amongst the grass, weeds and rushes of the woods and river-banks.

Across the river from my cottage the water meadows have the appearance of being covered with sheep, for the frosts have driven seaside swans inland for the winter. At a quick count 233 are grazing in one field, each with a grass intake that collectively will soon leave the field bare and fouled to the extent that cattle will refuse to graze there.

There is always something new to learn on this river. You spend your day wandering along the banks, peering into the water, believing that you know most things that go on. The contents of anglers' keepnets have a sameness – a lot of dace, a few roach and a chub. Of course there are the empty nets, but on the whole my fixed admiring glance knows what to expect, and it is this attitude that makes for surprises.

A new angler to my water fished a remote, overgrown back carrier. Later in the day my inquiry of 'What luck?' produced a pleased smile as the keepnet containing the usual species plus twelve wonderful golden tench was pulled splashing from the water. My eyes boggled. Tench! I had never before seen one caught on this river, yet here were a dozen from a small carrier connected directly with it. It explained the mystery of the occasional one that gets into my eel-trap, but it doesn't explain why we don't catch them on the main stream. Perhaps it is too fast, the gravel bed too solid.

I watched a shoal of chub sunning themselves in the slack water of a back eddy, suddenly realizing that two of them looked unusually big. They were 14-15 lb carp, ganging up with the chub for company, yet we have never caught one from the river. There are carp in various lakes that feed the river, so there is no reason why it should not hold some sort of carp stock. But except for the two I saw there is no evidence of their presence.

Until yesterday I believed that we had no bream in the upper part of the river, then last night one of those 14-year-old boys who are experts on all things fishy brought me a 1 lb 1 oz silver bream he had caught from my upper water. I put it into one of my aquarium tanks, promising him a positive identification the following day.

How careful you have to be with these youngsters nowadays. Say the wrong thing and they jump on you from a great height, never again to look on you with any sort of respect for your knowledge. Far better to say nothing and try to put on a wise and intelligent look that could mean anything.

The Water Authority are now going through their records seeing if perhaps their netting teams in the trout sections of the upper river can pinpoint the source of this fish. As for the fish itself, it was a true White Bream, with 22 branched rays in its anal fin and a scale count of eight in a straight line from its dorsal fin to its lateral line.

I welcome the tench; he is a fish of character and will fight his way to the net. The carp is perhaps misplaced in a river as fast as ours and probably he knows this better than we do. As for the bream, I hope that this fish is an isolated one that has slipped out of somebody's live bait can, and is not the nucleus of a shoal.

An awful thought! I hope nobody turns up at my cottage with one of those zanders. I fancy it would be a matter of 12-bore shotguns and hounds up to the North Country!

Part 4: Winter

Plastic in the Hatches

December came in with a rush of water, four inches in two days, and stopped the complacent thoughts that we didn't need to fix the lifting gear to additional hatches. Cattle moved out into low-lying water meadows were suddenly marooned on islands that had become the only ground above the water table.

It rained through the night, an unknown quantity until you pick up a feed bucket that was left out and find it half-full of water. That natural gauge leaves you looking at roofs and trees to see if they had added to the bucket's contents.

Slowly, during the day, the river rose. Rubbish that had accumulated on the gravel islands below Salisbury lifted off, the colour of the water was added to by a thousand streams off side-roads and ploughed fields.

A fresh crop of bottles – which nowadays seem to spring from nowhere – added a froth of glass to impounded back eddies. Then the Industrial Estate added a trimming of 40-gallon drums and discarded polystyrene packing. Solid blocks of some off-white buoyant plastic, half the size of a double-decker bus, came down like houseboats without windows.

They stuck in the hatches, disintegrated under pressure to a debris line down the centre of the current. All our hatches have been opened for the first time in two years, the first time we have had to look around for forgotten holes in the side of fields that have been blocked by boards which, now removed, help the run-off to the sea.

Alas, there is too much water for eel-trapping. The small domed eel-house was left marooned in this avalanche of water, while the afore-mentioned cattle were the cause of many favours asked, of borrowing waders by farmers leading them to higher ground. The weather forecast says further rain this afternoon and, even as I write, pot-marks begin to appear in the midst of the brown flood.

It seems likely that if it rises further we will claim salvage against British Gas. Their pipeline bridge that spans the Avon, put in when levels were at low summer drought, left a gap between the surface and lower side of the structure of nearly three feet.

Yesterday it floated off its stanchions so that two dragline diggers were hurriedly driven off the bank. The strange appearance of these two 60 ft jibbers, apparently marooned in midstream, with water washing over their tracks, is something not likely to be seen again.

Should today's rain persist and more of those little squiggly low pressure areas venture in from the Atlantic, there'll be more plastic in the hatches.

As a result of the flood and the fish being put off their feed, the coarse anglers have been having a couple of unproductive days. The oxygen content in the water has sunk to such a low that it is as much as fish can do to live, but there has been a run of salmon from the lower river to the redds: a continuous thread-like line of dorsals breaking the surface of the water below the hatches and then the movement sliding through the falling water with an acceleration as it reaches the upper levels.

There has been a spate of these salmon taking a couple of maggots, amusing the anglers by bending the rod for half an hour or so and then, suddenly finding their movement restricted, they sever the connection.

Early in November I was reminded of Mark Twain's character, Tom Sawyer, who, when he had to whitewash a fence, sold the right to do it to his pals and so turned what was an irksome job to profit. It was all very well in the beginning of last month when the stripping programme of some two thousand hen fish got under way. Inquisitive anglers peered over my shoulder, willing to get their hands wet with that slight tinge of blue around the edge, the same blue creeping up from their legs into their faces from standing in cold water.

There was never a shortage of volunteers. They tried the not quite ripe hen trout and milked the ripe ones, happy that they had fathered something that would grow into a fish. Then, as the month went on, there was this feeling of being avoided. They saw me coming from a distance and found that the fish were on the feed half a mile down-river, that it was necessary to get there before we could get at them. It was as if we were suffering from B.O.

With woollen socks on their hands, young river-keepers are learning that the coldest job is not in the chilly winds of February, but now, when the water is still in the mid-forties and prolonged immersion gradually lowers the temperature.

There is the surprise that strangers get when they see such a waterproof-clad apparition, some sort of Indian mystic with arms flapping and legs running on the spot, attempting to get warm. In the warmth of my fishing-room I switch on an extra bar of the electric fire and pour myself something stronger than tea in some sort of sympathy.

Gone are the days when hatchery troughs were full of trout eggs, when two pairs of keen eyes were necessary, with steady hand, to pick out the dead opaque egg from the live. Now, in fibreglass tubes, 100,000 eggs are stacked one on top of the other, and through a two-inch bed of gravel, clean, well-oxygenated water is fed to them in duplication of Nature's way.

Those hatchery troughs used to collect fungus on the spilled protein of a burst egg, till the decay spread through several square inches of hatchery space. You could dose these with malachite and partially dye the fungus green, killing it or nearly so. But in these incubators, the dead and the undisturbed protein get a dose of malachite in such an absolute fashion that one man can look after several million eggs.

This morning fish were hatching, alevins were swimming from the depths of unhatched eggs, struggling as if through gravel to the surface, 'til the free water above was a cloud of vigorous new life. They only need to lose a little of their yolk sac and follow the rising water to the outlet pipe, then they can swim away from the debris and leave the hatchery attendant with but a single minute of work disposing of the remnants.

Netting and Shocking

In these, the shortest days of the year, trout and salmon are spawning. To have both species spawn at the same time is bad planning on someone's part for they do great damage to each other's redds.

The salmon digs and softens up the bed, making ideal conditions for the smaller trout to come along and release the salmon eggs loose into the river where they are lost to the river's future stocks. I suppose it's been going on like this for thousands of years and there is little we can do about it.

Recently, when I was helping with a netting party on one of the chalk streams, several salmon were caught up in the nets. These salmon get very short shrift indeed – they never live to reproduce their kind. While I once thought that this was the thing to do, now that I deal with a mixed fishery I leave well alone.

These days out with the nets are always tremendous fun. Everyone gets on with their allocated jobs, be it the wheelbarrow along the bank or the wet end of the leading rope.

The net is pulled across the river and edged downstream with the current. Traditional snags are avoided with the benefit of long experience. We turn the bend and the corks go under as the heavily leaded net sags to take in an extra deep pocket of water. Then on, sweeping round the reverse side of the bend on to the shallows where nets have been hauled in by at least three generations of keepers and owners. Result – five pike and a dozen grayling.

Talking about netting grayling, somebody wrote recently in the angling Press criticizing the killing of these fish. It would do this gentleman no good at all to see the thousands of grayling that are killed each year on the chalk streams, for while roach, dace, perch and pike can be moved to other fisheries, the grayling suffers badly from even the smallest amount of handling. Anglers who have tried keeping grayling in keepnets will know the truth of this.

At least one Water Authority tries to tanker them to coarse fishing areas, but on the majority of chalk streams it's usually either a distribution of fish round the villagers or a hole in the corner of some wood. If these fish were not removed the river would soon become one giant grayling swim with little room for the trout, and if you are one of those who says 'What's wrong with that?' remember we are employees and it is the person who pays the piper who calls the tune.

It is interesting in these netting parties to weigh some of the larger fish. Twice in the last week grayling have been weighed-in at 3 lb 5 oz. When you think that these extra large fish come from water that is netted, then netted again, year after year, these efforts can't be so successful if they allow fish to survive the years necessary to reach that weight.

That goes for pike too. A stretch of our river, that in the 1600s was a canal, has at the bottom end a six-foot fall into an old lock and at the upper end an eel-trap that is run throughout the year. You might think that the stretch between these two obstructions would be free of any pike over three years old and weighing say three pounds.

Going down this not very wide stretch for the twentieth time to my knowledge in six years, the corks were thumped under by a good fish going into the net. We looked at each other and said 'salmon', but when the net was hauled, a 17 lb pike was thrashing in the belly of the net. How she had survived to that size we will never know.

The electric machine is more efficient in some conditions, but it is falling out of favour nowadays. It is still used on waters where the entire stock is changed each year, but on stretches of river that are semi-dependent on wild fish the electric machine is now under suspicion of perhaps doing more harm than good.

What seems to happen is that you run through a stretch of water seeing big trout up to six and seven pounds, plus the normal population of half-pound to one-pound fish.

The next time through, the very large fish seem to be missing and the whole average size seems to have slipped down a little, and so on with each successive trip through with the machine.

This might be a good trend on some waters that are hard-fished, but on the expensive trout streams a single large fish for one of our older anglers to sit behind for a week or so is of much more value.

The sad thing is that a good proportion of the smaller fish suffer from dislocated vertebrae as a result of charging full tilt into the field sent out by the electric machine. Is this what happens to the big fellows too?

The Survivors

When spring comes to the river, by order of Nature everything multiplies. A thousand eggs in a single action from the caddis fly produces — when the attack of its neighbours is over — perhaps two to succeed its parents. And so on down the line.

When you add all the different species of fly to the mallard chicks and those little black spots of life, the moorhens, then there is an abundance of food at this advance in the valley's year. Come autumn and the November, December frosts, everything is reduced to the adult, to those of each family that have survived the appetite of those that live on them. Then by an order in the 'Nature Council', families split up and wander farther than home boundaries in search of food – hence the sudden influx of mink with the winter winds.

A few weeks ago we had a single bitch on the trout stews that in passing brought our interests to the fore so that we enjoyed her life with us even to the end when we nailed her skin to the coal-shed door. Now more mink are harrying and flustering the trout stews and more than that, causing doubt whether it is good to be rid of them or not.

There's a big dog mink, as big as the village cat, black and shiny and with a zest for life. You've seen a rat-hole – if you hook your thumb and forefinger, that is the size of the average rat-hole – treble that in size and you have the round appearance of an adult dog mink. Yet that big black shining face and those pads disappear down the rat-hole and, like a ferret down a rabbit warren, flush the burrow's occupants like commuters out of a tube station at rush hour.

We poison our rats, we shoot 'em and we discourage them as all sensible people should, yet if a spoonful of trout food is left in the middle of a field with no apparent rat population, within a day they have found it and built up a small colony in the nearest soft earth.

Mink eat rats and fish and the question is, do we put up with the mink as an assistant rat-catcher or do we get rid of both with all the poisoning, shooting and trapping that that entails? Perhaps a mixture of both is the answer.

As the year moves on and the winter trips into place, a set of otter pads – feet marks in the river mud – begins to appear. Not the sort of pads we have got used to in the past, but something of unbelievable size.

If you see a badger-run and the row of four toes, you will see that the otter is of similar mark, except for one toe slightly backwards putting the four blobs out of line. The otter pad at the bottom of the garden, around the Water Authority's trout stews and my own trout farm, is almost three inches from end to end. A monster, you might say, of its species.

There used to be an old extrovert naturalist, Bill Mudge, who wandered the Itchen with binoculars grafted to the front of his chest and the round of the eye-pieces driven to form a permanent ring around his eyes.

Bill saw otters as big as grizzly bears; if pushed to the size and length of his imagination he would stretch his arms so wide that we couldn't fit an Itchen pike into the length. This present otter, up from the sea, is a Bill Mudge otter and I fear its appetite on the trout stews. Come to that, its water displacement would be a problem in the same place.

Moved on from somewhere else, with a growing appetite beyond youth, cormorants are in from the sea, as a gale-whipped coast lifts the waves on the white cliffs of the Isle of Wight. The gales toss the low-flying cormorant higher into the air, turn him inland and in the last week or so he has joined the general pestering of river-keepers with the heron.

Thank God he's not a night flyer, has not got the nocturnal habits of the heron and is a late riser, as most of us are.

Come the dawn, plus one hour, and the black goose-like figures fly upstream in close-packed coveys. They follow the twists and turns of the river, then, as they pass the first filled ponds, you can see them double-take as they spot water breaking over fish dorsal and nose. They do the sort of high rise flight that the RAF display teams call a bomb burst, tossing themselves into the sky then breaking to dispersal into individual stews.

But they are suckers with the need for a long take-off and when under water can be walked up on without caution. They are doomed before they begin to live a river life.

As I walk downstream from my cottage the river is a black and white quilt, the water covered with tufted duck. Then, as they rise and bank to sudden command, they are a picture of quiet organized life, a pattern of black and white uniformity of flight driven in from the coast. They join teal, mallard and, that pleasure to river watchers, the widgeon.

I watched a pike lying in eighteen inches of water, a fish of maybe eighteen or nineteen pounds – lying there without a tremble, and with such an unnatural stillness as to remind one of a water-logged piece of wood. Yet just above his dorsal fin there was a single tremor in his line as a piece of him bent this way and that to hold him (or her) there against the slight variation in current.

Last spring that pike would have been surrounded with all the youth of the feathered world dabbling in the surface above his head. Morsels to be picked as apples off a tree, while down there in the water there would have been more young dace than his appetite required.

I watched the pike for a while. Then suddenly there was a smoke-screen of mud that caught in the moving water and was swept away, leaving an expanse of brown dotted with Canadian weed and little else.

The time of the year has come when the full shopping basket has gone, bringing the hard times of having to look for a way to live. Only those who are fit and watchful will survive to see the spring next year.

A Thrilling Spectacle

The leaf is gone and the water has that much less debris to foul the weed-racks, gratings and eel-traps of the river. Jock, the hatchery manager, breathes thankfully that no longer does he have to remove that barrowful from his screens four or five times a day. In the absence of a salmon trap our river bailiffs, like the Indians of old, have been standing on the falls, net in hand, catching the salmon as they leap for the upper levels.

This poor salmon year has followed on into the winter. Those fish that have laid around in the estuary and lower part of the river have not been as numerous as we had hoped, so our heron-like bailiffs have not been as successful in the number they have caught. But there has been no shortage of salmon on the redds.

This annual spectacle never ceases to thrill me. It is like the gathering of the animals for the Ark. First in procession is the spawning female. In her shallow basin of gravel she gathers strength to turn suddenly on her side and with her flashing tail digs deep into the river-bed beneath her.

While she is so occupied, half a dozen bright red cock fish mill around, arguing with each other. A gigantic slab-sided fish of 30-odd pounds moves down the redd with a smaller rival held crossways in his mouth.

Then, at some hidden signal, one of the hen-attending cock fish charges forward to fertilize the eggs that she deposits beneath her.

These sticky fertilized eggs are then lifted backwards with more gravel on to the redd behind her or, as their stickiness dies away, wash away downstream to the waiting hordes.

There must be something pretty wonderful about the taste of a salmon's egg to cause all the agitation and greed that is shown by the fish that gather at this feast.

I have seen the jam that is made from a salmon's roe in some parts of Wales. I know how effective this is on the excited trout; almost under the hen salmon's tail they wait. Not big fellows, small fish around the half-pound mark. Their larger brothers are too busy with thoughts of their own spawning to gather at this time. They ignore the fighting of the cock salmon that goes on around them, moving only to each batch of fresh eggs as they are washed downstream.

Big cock grayling are pushed into the second rank, as are the dace and last year's salmon parr. In prime position in the slower water as it comes off the lower edge of the redd waits a shoal of portly chub. There, with all the time in the world, they dip to take each egg as it comes downstream. No arguing for them as to who takes which position, no chasing about after an egg that washes past. They lie in a certain order and seem to decide among themselves as to who takes what and when.

Eggs that survive to hatch in the redds will struggle towards the surface of the gravel as alevins in the early spring. If they are buried deep enough, their most vulnerable time to predators will be when they are wriggling through the gravel.

Even at this stage they are not completely safe. The cream-coloured mayfly larvae that forever hides from the light will dig its way down and feast on the young fish before it can reach the water above. Should it survive to lose its yolk-sac completely and live to feed in the flush of spring abundance, its enemies then will be too numerous to mention.

It is wonderful that any salmon survive to make the journey to the sea and return to spawn in our rivers.

But looking at it the other way, if one 20 lb hen fish carrying some 15,000 eggs were to spawn successfully and hide away every fertilized egg at just the right depth in the gravel, and every resulting parr were to migrate as a smolt to the sea, and each smolt should survive and return to this river, then from one breeding pair there would be hardly enough room in the river.

So perhaps it's as well that those fish gather to mop up the surplus eggs, otherwise the thought of a successful spawning year following a successful year would be too much to contemplate.

Pike in Retrospect

It's a cold, wet, miserable December morning, the air so full of damp that moisture drips from the trees in recurring showers as if the branches suddenly shook themselves.

There is a general feeling of lassitude and fishermen in the warmth of the cottage are reluctant to move out. Cars are parked in the lane with their windows misted up and a gentle continuous flutter from their exhausts.

Trying to get on with paper work in these conditions is like working in the middle of Paddington Station. Rods lean against the windows, haversacks are blocking the door. One angler sets our attitude to the day. He ventured out at first light with a packet of smelly herrings and came back with a story of a lost pike, a fish so big that there was a sense of relief in his tale that he didn't have to meet it face to face.

So, with a fresh batch of drinks from the kitchen, I give up all thought of work and add my voice to the continued stories of lost fish. There is nothing so memory-fixing as a fish hooked and lost. One that's been caught completes the cycle and leaves a memory from preparation to landing and I suppose in some cases right through to the frying pan and the sauce it was eaten with.

I have a friend who calls himself a culinary expert and dishes up the ordinary ingredients of a meal in exotic ways with exotic names so that you have no idea what it is you are eating.

When I've had the opportunity to dine in posh restaurants it has usually been at somebody else's request and I never quite have the nerve to read the more expensive dishes on the menu, let alone taste them.

Then the other day this friend, with much ceremony and unwrapping of small parcels, gave me pike to eat. I didn't know it was pike, otherwise I wouldn't have put the stuff in my mouth.

Covered in a delicious sauce it tasted like something that must have cost a lot of money. I sent my wife scurrying through Mrs Beeton's for the necessary recipes while I remembered all the tons of pike I had laboriously buried over the years.

At this time of the year, Test and Itchen river-keepers are out in force. Chain scythes have skinned weed 'til the bed of the river is bare, nets have swept downstream reducing pike populations to what the keepers fondly imagine is almost nil. Electric machines have been started up, plugs cleaned and a thousand small carriers that have harboured eggs from last spring are culled of most of their population of six-inch pike.

When I think of pike I have lost, it's always a small corner on the River Deben that is in my mind's eye, half a mile above Wickham Market where it's narrower and deep. Willows overhang, spaced regularly from no accidental planting.

On my leaves during the war I would scrape together the necessary livebait and sit in that one corner for many long days, joined by tank commanders from the nearby camp, seeking one particular pike that was something of a legend. It had been hooked by most of the anglers from the Glevering Camp and its size had grown with each successive telling of the story. It was not a fish to take the bait in a sudden diving run, but one of those fellows that sink the float slowly and go straight down until you can only catch a glimpse of the top of the float four or five feet beneath the surface.

Those of us who waited the prescribed time before tightening up would think that the bottom was well hooked, that one of the willow root clumps had grown out into deep water and was being used as a holt by this extra large and cunning pike.

The slow power and majestic movements of the fish from that moment on were described on the official bulletin boards of the Tanks Corps orderly room, the orderly-room sergeant and I being the two most addicted to that pike and the builders of the legend that surrounded it.

The story has a sad ending that doesn't affect my own feelings towards that bend in the river. A youngster from Wickham Market, all birthday tackle and clean boots, caught a 22-pounder from that area, and though it was dismissed as a minnow by those of us who saw it hanging in the butcher's shop, nobody caught a better one.

Caught Red-handed

In a countryside community, where within a ten-mile radius everybody knows everybody else's business, rumour travels faster than a telegram. There are pigeon-hole slots where each message is received by the person for whom it was intended and others get pleasure and enjoyment out of passing rumours on.

For some time at my 'receiver' I had been getting these bits of tittle-tattle about poaching from a neighbour's salmon pool, about big fish in and out of season hawked around the local pubs. There were sarcastic remarks from hoteliers hinting that the unofficial service of fish deliveries was better than the professional one.

We kept watch in a half-hearted fashion, never quite knowing the exact extraction spot. Then there was this boy, no taller or fatter than a milk churn, staggering down the centre of the local village and dragging, or rather walking by the side of, a 20 lb cock salmon, red as a beetroot with a three-inch kipe like a rhinoceros horn.

He was one of those boys who, on his way to school or home, recognized my transport and gave it passage as if it was royalty – a stand-by-the-kerb salute that does nothing for my ego. I recognized this as insurance being taken out against future or past river mischief.

On a previous poaching trip I had caught him with fresh-killed trout in his pockets, the soggy, dripping jacket filtering fish into the inner lining. I received his mother's pledge as to his future good conduct with a scepticism born of my own youth.

Now here he was with a parcel of fish that defied his ability to hide on his person. Despite his out-of-breath appearance, red face, cap rolled and stuffed into pocket, he saw me coming. Then there was this magic moment when every excuse passed through his mind and was shown on his face.

To drop it and run, to brazen it out – 'Found it dead' wouldn't have worked – it was still bent like a bow against the fingers in its gills, still with the half-light of life in its eyes. He withdrew his support and ran.

My companion in the car, a city person more used to town vandalism of broken windows and stolen cars, went into the realms of mirth associated with extremes of alcohol while I sent

the curse of river-keepers after the fleeing figure.

A bang on, the head with a roadside brick and the depositing of the dusty corpse in the car boot took but a moment. (The salmon, not the young villain.)

My temper was still bubbling and I remembered his parents' previous scolding as I drove. Turning right into the estate gate there flashed into my mind a mental picture of the hunted, cowering, chicken-house well raided, hounds baying at the door.

We let him be and went to the scene of the crime. Below a leaking set of hatches salmon vied with each other to run a near-dry sill, a water passage where in spring the wealth of water forms a Niagara of power, urging fish upstream in what to them is an easy passage.

In this low-water period they thrash through inch-deep shallows to narrow openings in weather-beaten oak hatchboard, broad backs out of water. With thirty miles of river passage behind them they are now vulnerable for the first time to local youth.

Another corpse, a hen fish of about 7 lb, the faded bloom of a sea-life still iridescent on her flanks, lay on the grass. A dozen village observers with an average age in the middle teens, stand passive-faced, disclaiming ownership of the fish, but eyes swivelling alive with interest as each new migrant flipped out of deeper water to join the others on the sill.

The watchers stood like some army from the past, each with a pole, the rudiments of a rod seven to eight feet long from the hazel bush, but without a line or reel between them. I phoned the Water Authority and explained about this barrier against migrating fish and complained of the fish diet the area must have been living on. Within a couple of hours each leaking crack had been amalgamated into one sizeable hole in that set of hatches so that the force of water gave the fish a sense of direction and allowed them on upstream.

Faster than I drove the two and a half miles round from those hatches to the salmon trap upstream, those released fish swam the threequarter-mile of river and filled the Wessex Authority salmon-keep with the fish necessary for this year's hatchery programme.

All this mucking about with salmon tends to rub off the glamour of the powerful fish and makes you take out your tackle and wish the months away to early spring. I use a 9ft 6in one-piece rod that has the power to stop any size of salmon – line and hook-hold permitting – but sometimes when there's a fish in the centre of the river and overhanging trees stop the bait from lying right, there's a need for a longer rod.

I tried one of 10ft 6in, again a one-piece, and a well-advertised carp rod of 11ft, but I got the feeling that I was close to coarse fishing and that somehow that bending tip would go on bending with anything over 20 lb. So I've given the 9ft 6in rod to the local tackle shop and asked them for a coat of varnish and will make it do for another season.

When Nobby caught his 3 lb 4 oz roach I wouldn't have been surprised if he had made a bonfire of all his rods, for what is there left when ambition is achieved?

In the early part of the year he got among the salmon and landed fish to 27 lb. I can still see his sickly grin when he took a quid from me at guessing the weight.

When coarse fishing got under way in mid-June he stood like a cormorant drying its feathers on the river bank, a forlorn picture of someone who couldn't bring himself to fish for dace when spoiled by his salmon catch – like a gambler moving from poker to ludo.

Then he was slowly weaned with this thought of perhaps a 2½ lb roach, a personal ambition to keep his angler's fire alive. When those irresponsible gods gave him this 3¼ lb roach he must have looked askance at his ambitions and wondered where to go next.

Rods and Guns

The start of the year has been a time of high water levels and moderate fishing temperatures, averaging 42 degrees Fahrenheit, never dipping and never lifting more than just a fraction on the thermometer.

Fish have come out constantly, as if that is what it is all about. Carp and barbel, that one associates with summer, have nibbled the occasional bait. A dace for every swim, a keepnet that does a tango under the bank while fish push on nylon netting and a feeding pike grabs at the lower end.

Why is it that roach seem to favour the cold water almost as much as the grayling and feature in the net as often as the trout? We have had spates of excited anglers to the cottage showing roach that should have weighed almost 3 lb according to the catcher's eye and yet dangled tantalizingly that fraction below the 2 lb mark.

The holiday period has been full of shooters, of ducks disturbed in backwaters so that they ploughed down and across the river. Widgeon and mallard, very few teal or tufted, and the occasional pochard coming in a red-crested skein. The movement of snipe, wisps that shunt in every direction across this fishing-room window, eddying like waders on a seashore.

Water meadows are still under water. They were meant to lift and drain, instead they sit there in stagnant grace with this multi-coloured population of waterfowl living on the fronds beneath the surface until the drowned meadows become polluted from so many aquatic fowl and eventually add to the nitrates and feed fish.

Across from this cottage, two umbrella-shaped anglers sit, fishing one of the downland high-level carriers that brings water from Salisbury to join the Avon above Downton. A line of guns crosses the meadows below them, and above them the advancing infantry of beaters, sticks banged into the ground and the multitude of sounds that constitute a countryman on his holiday adventure.

Snipe kicked out of the grass, a pheasant that began its ancestry in the bogs of China, and a small if reluctant teal are sent forward to join the splash of sound that is the artillery of the forward guns.

They are friends of mine — the advancing, the static and the anglers, each one playing his part in the occupation of the almost derelict lands of the semi-flooded water meadows. Anglers gleefully talk of feathered game that escaped, while pulling up the bank a keepnet that contains the big brownie which escaped in similar fashion last April or May.

A snipe that floated down, lodged itself on the weed-rack of the eel-trap, a bedraggled feathered river-valley friend, with a ring on its leg that said it was rung some eight years earlier. In a river valley it is only the river-keeper, and perhaps his hound, that survives a similar length of time.

I went out on one of the days over Christmas and joined the hunt that paraded in Salisbury Guildhall Square. I watched the Morris Dancers, then left and followed the hounds over the chalk downs. That would have been all right if it had just been me, but I gathered a tail of friendly fishermen who were not wise to country affairs.

There was none of this stand sedately in the fringe of a crowd and nod to the red-coated huntsman, but the passing of a bottle of Scotch that gave me a hint as to the occupation of the wader and waterproof-coated watchers. It was a sorry team that bundled into the back of a Land-Rover and then paused at each crossroads as the hounds milled around for scent.

We crossed the River Ebble at Odstock and dispersed downstream like a wave of uninterested spectators from the main fox-hunting fraternity and found a pair of spawning salmon in the lower Ebble. It was at this point that anglers distinguished themselves from normal country beings and showed that the wag of a fin is more important than a running fox.

Salmon running the Ebble, spawning in the fast water of an in-spate river, jumped at the concrete below the Bodenham dual carriageway. In attempting to run the hatches they dropped into the side channel in their fatigue and so lay there by the roadside in their tens and twenties, salmon taking a sudden chance at the passing water to put their nose out sideways and being whisked cartwheel-wise into the lower level.

Fox-hunting and Guildhall parties, Morris Dancers and country pursuits forgotten, we spend the day watching frustrated fish try to run twenty yards of fast water and then jump a hatch. Sea-trout by the dozen, small ones to ¾ lb dropping back into the alcove to rest, and then, having rested, finding there was no way to join the main flow without being washed back to the lower pool.

It was a repeat of the June elver, who climbs and then meets the current on the upper wall to start again and eventually migrate on. All those hunting people in their cars laughed at our fishing interests while they rambled across the downs, across the rough mud and kale, and spent a frustrating day.

We fishers watched the salmon and sea-trout and had the last laugh. Then, when the light was going from the sky, the huntsmen brought pack and followers back towards the boxes, found a brace of foxes almost as an afterthought from the reeds below Odstock Hospital, and sent them away across the hills towards Salisbury, brushes twisting in their haste.

The day was gone, salmon were still hurrying towards the hatch below the carriageway as tired as the hounds that were whipped off, as the horses that were boxed and the huntsmen who were still being offered Christmas cheer from more flasks than river-keepers ever see.

Fish-spotting Spaniel

The cold hard weather of January has thinned out anglers along the bank and, as always at this time of year, a few of my older friends have gone for ever. One of these friends was always accompanied by an old black spaniel. As often happens, over the years the two grew exactly alike in walk and appearance.

On fishing days the dog would make a quick survey of the river while his master was tackling up. Then, having assessed correctly the time needed for tackle to be assembled, he would walk to heel with head, like his owner's, turned towards the water, as they both weighed up the day's possibilities.

Early in their partnership the landing-net was done away with. The dog quickly learned the exact moment a fish was ready to be grassed and would mouth each one carefully from the water, avoiding the line.

The longer you have a dog the more human characteristics you attribute to it, and many's the time I have watched that old dog sitting behind the fisherman waiting for a suitable fish to rise. He had learned, it seemed, to ignore the small dace and the splashy grayling. He looked with interest across or behind him when a salmon jumped, but the angler swore that when a good trout quietly head-and-tailed, the old spaniel would nudge him to draw his attention to the rise!

I once had a dog that for years was a constant companion in my walks along the bank. She showed no interest in hunting rabbits – her pleasure was to watch fish. No particular sort so long as they moved and gave her room either to chase them along the bank or up the shallow water into the deeps.

I believe that bitch was equipped with polaroid eyes when she was born. She was taught to retrieve fish purely as an afterthought among the many other fishy things she did.

The netting parties were nothing without her and her 50-yard cord. At the netting site she was given the job of taking the first line across the river, the cord that pulled the ropes that allowed the nets to follow behind. When lunch came she would even ferry the beer and sandwiches to the far bank.

As a poacher-frightener she was supreme. I would leave her sitting a hundred yards down the bank while I did the final approach. At any sign of aggressiveness I would lift my hand and she would run ten yards towards us, then sit again, her appearance showing every sign of viciousness.

As for the poacher on the far bank out of my reach, she would at a command leap into the river and swim towards the offender, mouthing blood-curdling growls as she swam. A whistle when she was almost over would bring her back to my side and give me some bargaining power that always ended with the poacher moving on.

But in truth this gentle dog had more friends than it would be possible to count. She would carry a bucket of groundbait and ask no more than a friendly pat as a reward. She would swim out with the pike float and livebait and then spend the day anxiously waiting for some pike to take hold and struggle on its way in, for this she knew was the piece of excitement that followed that particular action.

In her latter days it pleased us to put a dace in a bath of water on the lawn. There she spent her last rheumaticky weeks following the fish round the circumference of the bath. She never tired of this until the day it was time for her to go.

One thing she never learned – she never could pick up an eel. In fact, in the darkened eel-trap when the eels were sliding over the rises she always stayed and watched from a distance.

As anglers grow old and their step gets as short as their wind, this doggie partnership is both delightful and pitiful. They grow old together and then one of them goes. The other then seems lost among the sedges and rushes of the river-bank on his own.

A White Wilderness

The valley is a wilderness of white and the river a black ribbon laid on a carpet of snow that blankets the valley from rim to rim, hides the rush and fills the iced-over dykes.

The waterfowl show up as black dots seeking food among the snowdrifts and the angler as a patch of green umbrella, with an even larger patch of disturbed snow showing black around him. Cold east winds drive across the water meadows, rattling frozen pellets of snow against waterproofs like number seven shot.

The willows are rimmed with a hard clear crust of ice that builds until it becomes heavy and falls into the river with a splash that for a moment makes one think an early salmon has become restless and has moved to view the world above it.

The surface water is cold, down to the edge of freezing. No fish moves near the rim of ice that fringes the river, no winter olives hatch to risk their short life without the sun as a guarantee of some warmth. Even the hardy trout in the stew with food ever available from a bucket make no effort to take the pellet floating on the surface. Only if the food is sunk do they open their mouths and feed without movement. This is as it should be, for when the river food supply is at its lowest, so should fish need it least.

Water from the chalk streams, some five degrees higher in temperature, enters and mingles with the main river. Fish accumulate in this warmer side current, not to feed, but to pass the time away until conditions improve in their home water.

In normal years these fish would have been in the deeps taking advantage of warmer water seeping through the gravel from the strata, but not this year.

The water in the strata has no pressure pushing from the hills. Springs haven't yet had the rain to break their bubbly chalky innards into life. As temperatures drop still lower the bed will freeze, ice will form among the gravel until its size lifts it to the surface.

When this happens, drifting ice on the surface is full of small particles of gravel and as this occurs when salmon and trout redds are loose and newly dug, great damage is done to the hidden eggs.

This freezing from the river-bed is something I have only seen on this river and then only when a certain set of circumstances arise. First the chalk hills in the upper part of the river valley guarantee water to the lower river in drought periods, therefore it is possible for the river to be running over a water table that is much lower than the river itself.

Consequently, when the river water drops down to freezing-point, the water on the bed of the river escaping into the strata finds a quiet corner and freezes, turning each pebble into a glistening diamond of ice.

The winterbourne demonstrates this freezing from the bed. When the stream has retreated down to the valley, leaving pools with gravel bars in between, a perceptible flow can be seen moving downstream. Then as temperatures drop to freezing, ice builds up on the lower end of each pool as the water enters the gravel.

Back on the main river, ice floating to the surface forms this floating carpet of gravel that we get in low-water winters. In three or four years' time, when salmon stocks from this year's spawning should be back into the river and we find them short, we will remember this year of the frozen redds and mark it down as the reason.

If we don't get our arithmetic right in adding up when fish are due back, we will make the same excuse for any year that doesn't come up to expectations in the next decade.

Winter Migrants

A cold east wind blows across the water meadows, seemingly straight from Siberia. It chills to the bone, freezes line to rod and makes the river-bank a most uncomfortable spot. But there must be worse places, for each morning sees fresh winter migrants moving into the river valley as the cold winds move them out of the north.

The Berwick swan looks small and out of place as he arrives from above the Arctic Circle to settle down among the larger mutes, while the curious cry of the Whooper swan sounds strange to the ear as he moves even further on to warmer climates.

An odd visitor is the petrel, something like a cormorant, but the size of a blackbird. Its home is the North coast of Scotland, yet these last few days have seen him driven inland to join the waterfowl of the river. How out of place they seem, and they must be, for this last week I have picked up three of their tiny bodies from among the riverside debris.

The bittern, still a stranger to us for most of the year, and as rare to England as barbel from a winter swim, arrives suddenly with the winter winds. He deserts his East Coast sanctuary for our warmer valleys, and perhaps this year he will stay on until the spring and breed.

The river is alive with every sort of duck — the little, tufted packs of widgeon and pochard. Even as I write and look out of the window, hundreds of mallard, disturbed by the fishermen, circle the water meadows in agitated flight.

They were joined this week by the red-breasted merganser. This large and handsome bird is not uncommon to the estuaries and rivers of the North, but it is only in the hard weather that he visits us to feed awhile on our dace and other fish.

I shall be glad when he is gone, but I think it will take a change of weather, perhaps even the approach of spring, to move him back to his Scottish lochs.

I watched a cormorant from the bottom of my garden as he hunted the river for a meal. What an easy task he made of it — a lift of the head and under the surface he slid to reappear about twenty yards on with an eight to nine-inch fish held crossways in his beak. He was successful half a dozen times as I watched, each time tilting his head and seeming to shake the fish down his throat.

The last time we ignored the cormorant, when storms at sea drove them inland for the winter, they built up a population that made a mile or so of the river useless as a fishery. They covered the banks with the whitewash of their droppings, but it was still with some regret that the 12-bore was taken from its case.

By standing still while the bird was on the surface, then walking up when it was under, the cormorant was stalked and shot, then brought home and taken to pieces. The stomach contents of any predator are always interesting, and none more so than the cormorant. Three salmon parr, four dace and a small roach were recognizable in the remains. What the rest of the mess consisted of we shall never know, but when you think that I watched this bird for only half an hour or so it is interesting to surmise what its total intake would be, fishing all the daylight hours. There is some indication in the fact that the Water Authority put 50p on every cormorant beak returned to them.

Our population of water-rail has suddenly multiplied. Almost with snow on their backs, they have flown down from the North during the hours of darkness.

This quiet, mobile little bird is a secretive friend to our anglers during the winter months. So is the little grebe. From frozen ponds and lakes, the little grebe has migrated to the ice-free river, though I'm blowed if I know how.

That he flies there is in no doubt, but in all the years I have been associated with river and country, never once have I seen him really get his legs up out of the water. A few years ago a keeper friend of mine recovered the body of a dabchick that had been 'leg-rung' somewhere in Holland, so I suppose that when they really try they must be quite good at flying.

Supply and demand, cause and effect – a shoal of dace migrate to fresh feeding because of a change in river circumstances and take with them the pike that has made his holt on the edges of the shoal. So it is with our bird migrants.

The peregrine falcon that has spent its summer months swooping over the duck on Minns Mere or off the cliffs of the Isle of Wight, now moves to easier pickings among the gathering wildfowl in this retreat from the winds and harshness of winter.

The Manor Ice-house

Hard frosts had frozen the moat round one of the old houses on the edge of the estate. The moat, more for show than to stop intruders, is a very shallow layer of water over a foot or so of silt.

The occupants of the house had seen dead fish under the ice so I was asked to go across and find out why. The reason was simple: no oxygen due to lack of flow, so my partner and I broke the ice and pulled it out on to the bank.

In a village this sort of activity does not go unnoticed and an aged, retired keeper came up with one or two suggestions as to what we should do with all the ice we had removed from the water.

One thing led to another and we were taken into a large wood nearby and shown the Manor Ice-house. In those far-off days before the turn of the century, labour was cheap and the estate staff that provided Manor sport held higher status in the local community than the farming staff or their management.

Fresh fish from the sea was an occasional thing, but the horse and cart that travelled the local villages after the twice-yearly netting of the rivers was something that could be relied upon to happen on time in March and October.

It was the river-keeper's job each year to fill the ice-house and enable both the Manor and the local people to keep their yearly issue of fish fresh for as long as possible.

As soon as the first winter frosts had a good hold on the land, certain hatches were opened into low-lying fields flooding them to a depth of three to four inches. When this water was well and truly frozen, it was broken up and carted to the ice-house. The house — which was a brick-lined pit going deep into the ground and roofed over with many feet of earth — had a floor two or three feet deep with cinders and clinker. On top of this the ice was packed in one-foot layers intermingled with straw.

The river-keeper told me that he could always manage to make that ice last throughout the summer months and sometimes well into the autumn.

The old keeper remembered the estate coming to a halt on the days when the netting parties were organized, and his job, as a boy, was counting and throwing the results of the netting into a cart. Nothing was wasted — dace, roach, chub and grayling were all issued out to the surrounding villages. The pike was looked upon as something a little better and was usually reserved for the day's helpers.

Nothing was weighed, but the skulls of many large pike were nailed to the old gentleman's garden shed. One of these measured nine inches across the flat part of the head.

Salmon were accounted a nuisance. Where the small chalk streams joined the main river, all sorts of barriers were erected to prevent the spawning salmon gaining access. It was no secret that gravid salmon were 'open season' any time after the end of October.

Two under-keepers were detailed off each year to 'wire' any salmon they saw trying to make a redd. Extra-strong rabbit wire (ten-strand) was used for this purpose and an extra-large type of bamboo was specially grown to produce the pole.

In this old keeper's records there are certain days in the middle of the 1880s when thirty to forty salmon were wired off the redds and buried under the rose bushes in the Manor House garden.

Nor were salmon the only fish to be treated in this fashion. In the April spawning time of grayling, the immobile hens were wired in their dozens. The cock grayling being a little more lively seems to have escaped this sort of end to his life.

Trout stocking was not the easy job it is today. The fry used to come by rail to the local railway station and be collected in barrels with a horse and cart. The route from the station had to be planned so that it passed various village pumps and small streams so that the water could be aerated en route.

The old keeper seemed to think that a lot of the fun had gone out of river work in these modern days.

The Secret Fishery

Do you bore your wife by stopping the car at every river bridge you come to when travelling in strange countries? Do you mentally fish each swim within sight and, if you know there are trout or salmon there, do you size up their lies and try to judge what fly would be most useful on that water? Or do you do as I do, wonder who fishes it and whether it is being made use of? Over the years I have brought many pieces of disused river and small lakes into use by various means. Of all this extra work, none has given me the same pleasure as some I took on about a year ago.

I was wandering with my dogs through some forest near my home when I came on a thousand acres or so of land that was pock-marked with bomb craters. Some of these were quite small and only a few feet deep. Others were huge and measured about forty yards across in any direction, their depths being dark and mysterious.

None of this was due to enemy activity but from RAF practice bombing during the war. In places the craters overlapped. Big or small, they had all become the home of the forest wildfowl, mallard springing into the air from every direction as we approached.

The water was heavily peat-stained, but carried nevertheless a very high insect population. Water-boatmen by the thousand and mosquito larvae were bobbing about all over the place. My mind said, 'Why not put a few fish in each hole?'

So in the early spring of last year I loaded a few hundred trout fry into the car and transported them in a dustbin through miles of boggy land, dibbing out twenty or thirty fry into each hole.

Later in the year Alex Behrents, owner of the fabulous Two Lakes Fishery at Romsey, put at my disposal some tench fry that he had netted out of his trout stews. These were ideal for my secret fishery in the forest. This time I was more selective, putting the tench only into the three largest craters.

For a month or so afterwards this project slipped into the background, the thought being in the back of my mind that I would go and see what it offered in a couple of years' time.

Then I wrote in *Angler's Mail* of the hen harrier which raised comment from my bird-watching friends in this area. I was approached by one gentleman who offered to show me where I could see a Montague's harrier. And he took me back into the forest among the bomb-craters.

After an hour of sitting and watching I wandered off to see if any small trout moved on the surface of the ponds and finding none in the early ones, moved on to do a complete circuit of each stocked pool.

At the largest one of all, a fisherman sat, completely out of place among the gorse and heather. He wasn't local, for after a hostile ten minutes of stilted conversation between us it eventually came out that walking that way in the summer months he had seen fish move near the surface (these were undoubtedly my trout fry) and had made the resolution to come back and fish at what he considered the proper time of the year, the winter.

He had caught nothing, neither had be seen anything, but then neither the trout nor the tench fry had had much time to grow. He promised me faithfully that he would not spread the whereabouts of my hundred small lakes and that he would return each fish he caught to the water.

But I have remembered all those anglers who stop their cars on river bridges, who gaze at fresh water wherever it is with inquisitive eyes, and all those ex-RAF types who will remember where their practice bombs were dropped, and somehow I think my ponds won't remain mine for very long.

A Memorable Salmon

February is upon us again and with it the start of the salmon season.

It's strange the way a river gets into your mind. Between June and March I see the river full of coarse fish of one sort or another, then suddenly, at a given date, my mental picture changes and large silvery shapes mingle with the coarse fish shoals.

February fish are rare and tend to be caught on opening day. Having moved upstream during the preceding month and found themselves a comfortable niche, they are suddenly awakened with flashy baits and gaudy flies. These stragglers go into the book early, then we wait for the early trickle from the sea to replace them.

My earliest ever fish came by accident. With no thoughts of salmon in mind I wandered out in early February, dogs at heel on exercise. Of course I took a rod because I walked the dogs the river-bank way. Up past the bathing pool, across the head of the weir and past the old iron bridge, watching the water as I went.

Down in the quiet, on the edge of the current, something showed silver. It looked like a roach, but what was making it so difficult to distinguish was that it had a head, then a black gap, then a tail. It was a good roach, possibly close to 2 lb. As I watched, the tail would suddenly wake into life and thrash wildly.

Then I realized that this condemned fish was in the mouth of a good size pike and that the black shadow hiding its middle was the pike's mouth.

I stayed and watched the fish being turned without any apparent movement from the pike. I saw the head go in and the tail slowly vanish. A half-hour job from first to last.

I took off the small Devon that was on the rod and replaced it with the largest double-jointed yellow plug you ever saw.

I thought that if I waggled this in front of our non-hungry

pike, at least I would have the fun of an anticipated take, even if I did frighten the life out of him in the process.

I cast out into the current to bring the bait up into the dead water, then everything went solid in midstream. A tug to free it and a most magnificent spring salmon heaved itself into the air.

A kelt might have been possible on such a large bait and at such a time of the year. A three-inch Devon or a five-inch golden sprat should have been the bait had I had the faith to fish for salmon so early. But there was no time for thought now. The fish turned and ran downstream over the weir, down the bathing pool, past the springboard, turning deep in the water on the far side. I had come without a gaff and was far from help, no matter how hard I could shout or whistle. If I lost this particular fish who would believe a tale of one that got away?

But the hooks held firm and in quite a short time I brought him near the back. With a handkerchief round my hand I grasped him by the wrist of the tail and attempted to lift him out. He shot off downstream with renewed life. I don't think he had had any idea that he was hooked until that moment.

With great vigour he demonstrated why spring salmon are so eagerly sought on this river, why tales of misfortune are more often told than bodies shown. At last he came in and I lifted him on to the bank.

I was aware that this was the earliest salmon ever caught in the county and as such must be of interest to the Water Authority officials. So I phoned the story through.

The man at the other end snorted. 'A large kelt,' and, despite my assurance to the contrary, didn't seem to be convinced. On the other hand, my employer, with visions of his dinner table in mind, was quite happy. A large knife was produced and the fish shared according to his wishes.

The man from the Water Authority obviously had second thoughts, for later in the afternoon he turned up complete with a television camera crew to take a shot or two of the corpse, but alas, he was too late, and he remains to this day unconvinced that that fish really was a springer.

An Unhappy 'Love' Story

The end of another shooting season and suddenly the surviving cock pheasants come out of hiding, strutting around in the knowledge that they are safe to parade their glossy spring coats. When I game-keepered I felt sorry as the year went on, to see the end of the birds so carefully cultivated and then so desperately hunted to oblivion.

I get the same feeling now with my trout. You watch the golden stream of eggs levered from the belly of the gravid trout, see them fall into a bowl, and then, over the course of weeks, become the home of a live embryo inside a living sac.

Watching it through its various stages of life, sitting over it and guarding its existence through to the point when it's knocked on the head, gives you a feeling of despair for such a short life. But if it were wild and lived a free life would it fare better? I'm not certain.

Outside the fishing-room window, a straggly ribbon of water runs at the speed of a galloping steer past this house and back into the main river a hundred yards away. In a small eddy beneath a scruffy elm with trailing ivy dragging scratches on the surface, are two salmon — a cock and a hen.

He, a once proud thirty-pounder, is now dressed in white 'mink' with barely a part of his original scaly coat free from the creeping smudgy mass of fungus, with a greyish undercoat covering his eyes to blindness and his dorsal fin to disintegration.

His bride is less infected though in one way more handicapped. Her tail is like the remnants of a flag that has been waved in the wind too long — ragged and formless, a beaten stump that has lifted half a ton of gravel a dozen yards downstream.

They came upstream in the early spring and refused the blandishments and invitations from a thousand whirling baits.

They sat with worms and prawns hung deliberately in their line of vision, then when the season acknowledged as being for them alone ended, they had refused the baited hook designed to catch barbel.

As the year ebbed and the store of fat tied up within them died, the fish moved out of the main river and tested the loose gravel under the bridge alongside this cottage. Satisfied that here was going to be the honeymoon suite, the hen set up house and waited for that moment when her eggs lost their lesions and became ripe.

Endowed with all the patience in the fishy world, contented with her lot and saving her energy for the trials ahead, the hen ignored her consort and, in doing so, seemed to send him daily into mistaken wild activity.

Within view of the fishing-room window he would surge on a downstream beat, sending waves into the margins and frightening the life out of friendly chub that wanted nothing more than the quiet life of sideways drift into the shadow of the trees.

As his milt advanced, so the kipe on his lower jaw grew and formed a socket in the upper part of his beak, making a white mark that showed his coming and going like the ensign on a battle cruiser.

He took to charging with mouth agape and dorsal fin shark-like out of the water, so that even the friendly dabchick moved out to quieter places. Expending his energy to waste it seemed, while his bride sat quiet, reserving hers for the bridal redd.

From September to Christmas we watched him daily, watched the tiny portion of fungus take hold just forward of his shoulder, watched the pounds slip off his frame and the width grow narrow so that he became more slab than broad of hulk.

A couple of canoes coming that way chased them back to the main river and we lost them for a while in coloured water. But come the end of December they spawned and spent a happy week, she digging while he played with the boys below her.

He was fighting, harrowing and mating and gradually pulling the coat of fungus across his shoulders, over the head, back towards the tail and round the vent.

He has lain in the garden pool for five days now, in a 'dead,' sick condition, while she is recovering fast by an injection of energy from the residue of the eggs she held within her. Perhaps it is a thousand unreleased drops of life now redigested that have caused her to mend and put a silver sheen back into her ragged scales.

He, lacking the will to live, will be found by some passing mink and harried into putting his nose ashore where his weakly waving tail will put him beyond return to deep water. He will suffer the indignity of being nibbled by brown rats who a few short months ago would not have dared to swim in his presence.

A slow lingering end that Nature condemns him to while offering a chance of life to lesser-sized members of his kind spawned less wastefully. Perhaps it would have been better to have lived a short well-fed life.

On one of those wet blustering days that we have been blessed with during this early part of the year, I walked off into the New Forest to catch the pleasure from all those cascading streams that cross and cross again through these 90,000 acres of wood and moorland.

On every gravel stretch, families of sea-trout grubbed like pigs, showing the strength of their work by the damming of those fast, peat-stained waters.

There is a country harvest gleaned from the middle of these quiet acres by the roving families of New Forest gypsies. Feasts of spawning sea-trout from blackened pots in secret camps on the edge of the old sheep droves.

I met such a group, super-polite in their attitude to those they think of as authority and offhand to the point of rudeness to those who would interfere.

A gorse bush was brought down by willing hands through the redds to another gorse bush that strains the water and holds the fish – ready-to-hand 'nets' that aren't obvious to the ordinary eye, and available at the stroke of an axe.

I am allowed to watch, but not to photograph, and I see them spoil fish by throwing them into dirty fertilizer bags for transport home.

It's part of the New Forest scene and not something to be worried about. It has been the same for a thousand years.

The Black Sheep

When it comes to the big angling organizations I often wonder how their thousands of members are 'organized' into obedience, how the greedy are kept within bounds. My own syndicate, well policed by country lads, is not without its black sheep. In fact just at the moment there seems to be a shortage of the white sort.

We have a rule, pointed out on joining, that no guests are allowed, but fishermen tend to be lonely creatures. They seem to need someone to hold their hand or buy them a pint, and so they evolve ways of getting round the rules.

They bring their children down and pretend to teach them to fish. They could hardly be called guests or additional rods. The wife sitting there knitting, just happens to be looking after the leger rod. You can't leave her at home and really she's not taking up any space!

I have returned money to the awkward sort, had it pushed back through the post and carry on a running battle to make them stick to what few rules we have. On my desk I have an angling organization's handbook of around sixty pages outlining fisheries, river boundaries and a few rules which are applied to thousands of the keenest sort of angler. From conversations with the people involved, it would seem that they have fewer problems – and fewer rules – than I do. But I don't get to the state of armed aggression that one of our river-keepers reached. Somebody kept stealing his boat from the bottom of the garden, pinching it in the night when dog and keeper were both asleep.

He loaded both barrels of his 12-bore and with elaborate strappings, fastened it through the bathroom window and facing downstream, with a line attached to both triggers hidden in the grass.

He took the precaution of cutting the pellet end from the cartridge and allowed for some deflection. What he didn't make allowance for was the noise of two barrels from the gun exploding in the bathroom at two o'clock in the morning.

It woke the children screaming, his wife wouldn't talk to him for a week, and still his boat was cut loose and found a mile downstream waterlogged. But the idea was successful in as much as the boat-stealers didn't try it again.

It must be difficult not to feel pleased about catching a 29 lb salmon, a fish well above the average size. When the gods allocate such things their fingers pass many names before resting on the lucky angler.

So put yourself in the position of such an angler last week. The river in flood, the normal high-level salmon lies difficult to cast to and, even worse, difficult to wade within casting distance.

The river has been fishless, netsmen at the mouth talking of dole money and passing the hat round. Then suddenly, a 29 pounder was hooked and successfully grassed – and the rules of the fishery became involved.

You pay £25 for the right of two of you to fish one beat one day a week. Well, that's cheap enough. Then the snags: each fish you catch you must pay for at the going market rate and never is the rate higher than for this first fish of the season.

There must be a temptation to exaggerate the weight perhaps to your friends, but when you have to pay for that exaggeration, what a brake on the enthusiasm!

Work out 29 lb at roughly £2.50 per pound and there must be some temptation to hide it in the boot of the car, to throw it back in the river, to do anything but fork out about seventy quid for the privilege.

It makes salmon fishing even more of a lottery and brings the wishes of the angler into direct conflict with his pocket.